Junior Great Books

BOOK ONE

Junior Great Books®

3
Relationships
Kindness
Confidence

BOOK ONE

Great
Books
Foundation

Copyright © 2014 by The Great Books Foundation

Chicago, Illinois

All rights reserved

ISBN 978-1-939014-50-4

8   9

Printed in the United States of America

Published and distributed by

THE GREAT BOOKS FOUNDATION
A nonprofit educational organization

233 North Michigan Ave, Suite 420

Chicago, IL 60601

www.greatbooks.org

CONTENTS

Kindness

Confidence

INTRODUCTION

Welcome to Junior Great Books! In this program, you will be reading stories and discussing your ideas about them. Before you begin, here are some important things to know.

The stories in Junior Great Books will make you wonder about things. You might wonder what a word means, why an author told the story this way, or why a character does something.

You will start by reading along as the story is read aloud. Your teacher will ask you to think of questions you have about the story while you read. Any question you have about the story is worth asking.

At the end of the story your teacher will ask you all to share your questions about it.

Your teacher will write down all the questions so everyone can think about them. Some questions can be answered right away. Others will be saved to talk or write about later on.

Next, everyone reads the story again. During the second reading, you will do some activities that help you think more about the story's meaning. You might take notes, share your thoughts about the story with a partner, or act out scenes from the story.

When it is time for discussion, everyone will sit in a circle or square so you can see and hear one another. Your teacher will start the discussion by asking a question about what the story means.

The discussion question will have more than one good answer. Your teacher isn't trying to get you to give the "right" answer to the discussion question. It is all right if people disagree about the best answer.

During discussion, your teacher will ask more questions to help you say more about your ideas. You might be asked to go back to the story to find evidence for your ideas or explain more about what you mean. You can also ask questions about your classmates' ideas, and agree or disagree with what they say.

At the end of the discussion everyone will understand the story better, even if you all have different ideas about it. This kind of discussion is called a Shared Inquiry discussion. "Inquiry" means exploring many different ideas or answers to a question. "Shared Inquiry™" means you are exploring together.

After discussion, you may do other activities that help you think more about the characters and ideas in the story. Your teacher may have you write or draw something. You may read a book that connects to the story you discussed. Or you may do a project with a group or with the whole class.

Even after the class is done working on a story, you might keep thinking about it. Every time you ask a question or have a discussion about a story, you are learning to think more deeply about what you read. You are also learning how stories work and what kind of stories you enjoy. You are becoming a great reader.

Dos and Don'ts in Discussion

DO
Let other people talk, and listen to what they say.

DON'T
Talk while other people are talking.

DO
Share your ideas about the story. You may have an idea no one else has thought of.

DON'T
Be afraid to say what you're thinking about the story.

DO

Be polite when
you disagree
with someone.

DON'T

Get angry when
someone disagrees
with you.

DO

Pay attention to
the person who
is talking.

DON'T

Do things that make
it hard for people
to pay attention.

Shared Inquiry Discussion Guidelines

Following these guidelines in Shared Inquiry discussion will help everyone share ideas about the story and learn from one another.

 Listen to or read the story twice before the discussion.

 Discuss only the story that everyone has read.

3 Support your ideas with evidence from the story.

 4 Listen to other people's ideas. You may agree or disagree with someone's answer, or ask a question about it.

 5 Expect the teacher to only ask questions.

Theme Introduction

Relationships

In this section of the book, you will read about different kinds of relationships. Thinking about these stories, and about the connections you have with people in your own life, will give you new ideas about what it means to have different kinds of relationships.

Important Questions to Think About

Before starting this section, think about your own relationships:

- What are some examples of good relationships in your life?

- Why are your relationships important to you?

Once you have thought about your own experiences with relationships, think about this **theme question** and write down your answers or share them aloud:

What do you need to have a good relationship with someone?

After reading each story in this section, ask yourself the theme question again. You may have some new ideas you want to add.

· *What Grace liked best was stories.* ·

BOUNDLESS GRACE

Mary Hoffman

Grace lived with her ma and her nana and a cat called Paw-Paw. Next to her family, what Grace liked best was stories. Some she knew and some she made up. She was particularly interested in ones about fathers—because she didn't have one.

"You do too have a father," her ma said when she caught Grace talking that way. "I must have told you a hundred times about how we split up, and your papa went back to Africa. He has another family now, but he's still your father, even though he doesn't live with us anymore."

Well, that wasn't Grace's idea of a father! She wanted one like Beauty's, who brought her roses from the Beast's garden in spite of the dangers. Not one she hadn't seen since she was very little and only knew from letters and photographs.

And in her school reading books Grace saw that all the families had a mother and a father, a boy and a girl, and a dog and a cat.

"Our family's not right," she told Nana. "We need a father and a brother and a dog."

"Well," said Nana, "I'm not sure how Paw-Paw would feel about a dog. And what about me? Are there any nanas in your schoolbooks?"

Grace shook her head.

"Do I have to go then?" asked Nana.

"Of course not!" Grace said, hugging her.

Nana hugged her back. "A family with you in it is a real family," she said. "Families are what you make them."

14

Then one day when Grace got home from school, she saw a letter on the table with a crocodile stamp on it. Grace knew it must be from Papa, but it wasn't Christmas or her birthday.

"Guess what!" Ma said. "Your papa sent the money for two tickets to visit him in Africa for your spring vacation. Nana says she'll go with you if you want. What do you say?"

But Grace was speechless. She had made up so many fathers for herself, she had forgotten what the real one was like.

Grace and Nana left for Africa on a very
cold gray day. They arrived in The Gambia in
golden sunshine like the hottest summer back
home. It had been a long, long trip. Grace
barely noticed the strange sights and sounds
that greeted her. She was thinking of Papa.

I wonder if Papa will still love me? thought
Grace. He has other children now, and in
stories it's always the youngest that is the
favorite. She held on tightly to Nana.

Outside the airport was a man who looked a
little like Papa's photo. He swung Grace up in
his arms and held her close. Grace buried her
nose in his shirt and thought, I do remember.

In the car she started to notice how different everything seemed. There were sheep wandering along the roadside and people selling watermelons under the trees.

And when they reached her father's compound, there was the biggest difference of all. A pretty young woman with a little girl and a baby boy came to meet them. Grace said hello, but couldn't manage another word all evening. Everyone thought she was just tired. Except Nana.

"What's the matter, honey?" she asked when they went to bed. "You've got a father and a brother now, and they even have a dog!"

But Grace thought, They make a storybook family without me. I'm one girl too many. Besides, it's the wrong Ma.

The next day Grace started to get to know Neneh and Bakary. The children thought it was wonderful to have a big sister all the way from America. And Grace couldn't help liking them too. But she had to feel cross with someone. Grace knew lots of stories about wicked stepmothers—*Cinderella, Snow White, Hansel and Gretel*—so she decided to be cross with Jatou. I won't clean the house for her, thought

Grace. I won't eat anything she cooks, and I won't let her take me into the forest.

Jatou made a big dish of savory benachin for lunch, but Grace wouldn't eat any. "I'm not hungry," she said.

"She's probably still getting over the long flight," said Jatou.

When Papa came home from work, he found Grace in the backyard. He sat beside her under the big old jackfruit tree. "This is where my grandma used to tell me stories when I was a little boy," he said.

"Nana tells me stories too," said Grace.

"Did she ever tell you the one about how your ma and I came to split up?" asked Papa.

"I know that one," said Grace, "but I don't want to hear it right now," and she covered up her ears.

Papa hugged her. "Would you like the one about the papa who loved his little girl so much, he saved up all his money to bring her to visit him?"

"Yes, I'd like that one," said Grace.

"Okay, but if I tell you that story, will you promise to try to be nice to Jatou? You're both very important to me," said Papa.

Grace thought about it. "I'll try," she said.

The next day they went to the market. It was much more exciting than shopping at home. Even the money had crocodiles on it! Lots of the women carried their shopping on their head.

Then they went to a stall that was like stepping inside a rainbow. There was cloth with crocodiles and elephants on it and cloth with patterns made from pebbles and shells. And so many colors!

"We can choose cloth for Grace's first African dress," said Papa. Grace and Nana spent a long time choosing. No one was in a hurry.

The days of Grace's visit flew by. She played
in the ocean with her brother and sister, and
she told them a bedtime story every night.
She told all the stories she knew—*Beauty and
the Beast, Rapunzel, Rumpelstiltskin*. It was
amazing how many stories were about fathers
who gave their daughters away. But she didn't
tell them any about wicked stepmothers.

Sometimes Ma called from home
and her voice made Grace feel
homesick. "I feel like gum,
stretched out all thin in a
bubble," she told Nana. "As if
there isn't enough of me to go
around. I can't manage two
families. What if I burst?"

"Seems to me there *is*
enough of you, Grace," said Nana.
"Plenty to go around. And remember, families
are what you make them."

Soon it was their last evening and there was
a big farewell party at the compound. Grace
and Nana wore their African clothes and Grace
ate twice as much benachin as everyone else.
"Now you really might burst," said Nana.

On their last morning Papa took Grace to see some real crocodiles. "This is a special holy place," he said. "The crocodiles are so tame, you can stroke them."

"Not like the one in *Peter Pan!*" said Grace.

"No. These are so special, you can make a wish on them," said Papa.

Grace closed her eyes and made a wish, but she wouldn't say what it was.

Later at the compound Grace asked Nana, "Why aren't there any stories about families like mine, that don't live together?"

"Well, at least you've stopped thinking it's your family that's wrong," said Nana. "Now, until we get back home and find some books about families like yours, you'll just have to make up a new story of your own."

"I'll do that," said Grace, "and when we're home again, I'll write it down and send it to Jatou to read to Neneh and Bakary."

The whole family came to see them off at the airport. Grace was sorry to say goodbye to her new brother and sister and even to her stepmother. But leaving Papa was hardest of all.

Waiting for their plane, Nana asked Grace if she had thought any more about her story.

"Yes, but I can't think of the right ending," said Grace, "because the story's still going on."

"How about they lived happily ever after?" asked Nana.

"That's a good one," said Grace. "Or they lived happily ever after, though not all in the same place?"

"Stories are what you make them," said Nana.

"Just like families," said Grace.

23

· *The scarecrow had no head.* ·

THE SCAREBIRD

Sid Fleischman

One time a lonely old farmer jammed some old clothes full of straw and put up a scarecrow.

But the scarecrow had no head.

"Just keep the cuss-hollering birds out of the corn patch," said the farmer. "You don't need a head for that."

It was true. Crows and blackbirds circled the long-armed, long-legged scarecrow and kept at a safe distance.

But as the first days of spring passed, the farmer—called Lonesome John by the folks in town—grew uneasy. Every time he looked up from his chores, there stood that headless scarecrow.

And after supper, when he sat on the porch and played his nickel-plated harmonica, there against the fading sun stood the headless scarecrow.

"If that's not the most fearsome sight I ever saw, it'll do," said Lonesome John in a loud voice. With his family gone and his old dog Sallyblue buried in the pasture, he had no one left to talk to but himself.

"That scarebird's enough to give a man the cold creeps."

The next morning Lonesome John hunted up an old pillowcase and stuffed it with straw. He used house paint to dab on a pair of yellow eyes. A hole in the pillowcase would do for a mouth.

He sauntered to the corn

patch and fixed the head to the neck of the scarecrow.

"Does that face suit you, Scarebird? You look like sunshine on stilts with them yeller-paint eyes! Well, make yourself at home."

The next day, when Lonesome John went out to start up his tractor, he gave a wave. "Mornin', Scarebird! I slept like a pine log. How about you!"

And in the evenings, when he sat on the front porch playing his nickel-plated harmonica, he felt almost as if the scarecrow could hear every note.

"See you tomorrow, Scarebird!" he'd call out when he went in to bed.

Lonesome John was sleeping like a pine log when he was awakened by wind banging the barn door. He'd heard wind before, and went back to sleep. At daybreak, with the wind now howling and shrieking in his ears, he jumped out of bed.

The scarebird!

He looked out the window. There stood the scarecrow, face to the wind, holding his ground. Lonesome John grinned.

"I figured you were a goner, Scarebird!"

But when he squinted his eyes, he saw the wind was plucking straw from the scarecrow's cuffs and carrying off its hands and feet.

Lonesome John rushed outside with a pair of shoes and work gloves, and his pockets full of fresh straw. Within minutes he had replaced the straw in the cuffs, put the gloves on, and laced the shoes up tight.

"You're good as new, Scarebird, and a little better." And then he added, "Ain't you all dressed up! Those are my town shoes, but I hardly go to town anymore so you're welcome to them."

The wind whisked itself away. The days turned hot. Before long the sun was rising like a blowtorch at full blast.

"Mornin', Scarebird. Looks like another scorcher today."

Every time Lonesome John glanced up from
his farm chores, there stood the scarecrow
bareheaded under the flaming sun. He
remembered how ol' Sallyblue used to head
for the shade under the house on summer days
like this.

"Scarebird, you need a hat," he called.

He picked out his wide-
brimmed straw hat, his
town hat, and set it on the
scarecrow's head. He pulled
the brim low over the
sunflower-yellow eyes.

"That's my bettermost
hat, but you're
welcome to it."

The hot spell
passed, the
evenings cooled off,
and after supper Lonesome John sat on the
porch playing old tunes on his nickel-plated
harmonica.

"See you tomorrow, Scarebird."

But dark clouds tumbled in during the
night, and when Lonesome John awoke he

could smell rain. And he heard the windows chattering like baby rattles.

"It's going to rain blue thunderbolts!"

He rushed outside with his yellow slicker, pulled the arms of the scarecrow through the sleeves, and threw the hood over the wide-brimmed hat. When he had the rain gear buttoned, he looked up at the swollen clouds.

"Yes sir, blue thunderbolts. Won't do to have you get soaked through and mold up, will it?"

The earth was drying out when Lonesome John hunted up his old checkerboard. He set an apple box in front of the scarecrow and opened the board.

"How about a game of checkers? I ain't played since the boys left home, so I'll be a mite rusty. You go first."

Lonesome John moved a checker for the scarecrow and then one for himself. Before long the game was far along and Lonesome John was in deep concentration.

"Your move, Scarebird."

Lonesome John hardly noticed the time pass. "King me, Scarebird! I ain't licked yet!"

Then a shadow fell across the checkerboard.

He looked up and saw a young man in worn jeans standing there, barefooted and bareheaded.

"Howdy, sir. Folks in town said you might need a hired hand."

"I get along by myself," answered Lonesome John.

"Yes, sir."

Lonesome John wanted to get back to the checker game, but the stranger looked foot-weary and hardly more than sixteen or so.

"You legged it all these miles? Didn't they tell you it's so far to my place that crows pack a lunch before setting out? If you're hungry, you'll find bread and side meat in the kitchen."

"Thanks."

"And open a can of peaches while you're at it."

Lonesome John resumed the checker game, though his mind was no longer on it.

The hired hand finished his meal. "I'll chop you some stove wood before I head back."

"Just a stick or two will be fine."

Lonesome John finished up the checker game, but felt foolish with a stranger looking on. He was careful not to talk aloud to the scarecrow, but he thought, "Seems like a nice enough lad, don't he, Scarebird?"

When he returned to the back porch, the hired hand was using a whetstone on the blade.

"The axe needs sharpening."

Lonesome John grinned a little. "It usually does. Wouldn't mind some help with the weeds, if you'd care to stay a day or so."

"Glad to. My name's Sam."

"There's a room off the barn. You can sleep there."

After supper Lonesome John sat on the
porch, but he didn't play his nickel-plated
harmonica. He'd feel uncomfortable with a
stranger about the place. He gazed off at
the scarecrow standing lonely under the
darkening sky.

"See you tomorrow, Scarebird," he muttered
softly.

Sam spent the morning with the hoe,
working away steady as a clock.

"He's raising blisters on his hands,"
Lonesome John said to himself, and pulled the
work gloves off the scarecrow.

"Put these on."

"Much obliged, sir."

"My name's John. John Humbuckle."

It took more than a day or so to catch up
with the weeds. The hired hand stayed on,
working under the hot sun without a hat on
his head.

"Scarebird," said Lonesome John, "you won't
mind if that young feller borrows your hat."

"Thank you kindly," said the hired hand.

"You from someplace?"

"Used to be."

"Where are your folks?"

"We graved and prayed 'em when I was a
little kid."

When the weeding was done, Sam hung up
the hoe and pulled off the gloves and hat. "I'll
head back."

Lonesome John scratched his neck. "I've been meaning to clear that thornbush in the orchard, if you'd care to stay on a day or so."

"Sure thing."

"Them thorns are meaner'n fishhooks. You'd better wear shoes."

It was raining at first light. Lonesome John pulled the shoes off the scarecrow, then the yellow slicker.

"The boy'll be ever so grateful, Scarebird."

It was almost a week before they had the last of the thornbush grubbed out and burned.

35

After supper, the hired hand joined Lonesome John on the porch. "I never saw a scarecrow with yellow-painted eyes. I had a dog once with yellow eyes. He was a mighty good friend. I'll never forget him."

"That's the way it is with good friends."

"Job's done. Time for me to clear out tomorrow." And then Sam pulled a harmonica out of his pocket and began to play a joyful tune.

Lonesome John was silent for a long time, listening. Then he said, "It's time to start harvesting the crops, if you want to stay on a day or so, or a week or so."

"Yes, sir. Sure thing."

Lonesome John had been fingering the
harmonica in his own hip pocket like an itch
that needed scratching. Now he pulled it out
and smiled broadly. "Do you know this tune?"

He began to play, working his right hand
like a bird's wing to polish up the notes. When
he was finished, Sam tapped his harmonica.
"Do you know this one?"

They played, one after another, until full
dark. When it was time to turn in, John
Humbuckle looked over at the scarecrow for
a long moment and then turned to Sam.

"Do you play checkers?"

"Oh, Peerless Ginger Cat! Catch a fish for me!"

Chin Yu Min and the Ginger Cat

Jennifer Armstrong

Many years ago, in a village near Kunming, there lived an official of the government named Secretary Chin. In his house by the lake were the finest lacquer bowls, lettered scrolls of the sheerest paper, and many, many strings of cash. Secretary Chin was very prosperous.

The wife of this man, Chin Yu Min, felt that this prosperity was only what she deserved. She was proud and haughty, and she made her servants perform impossible and meaningless tasks—such as collecting incense smoke in a bamboo cage or teaching carp to strut like roosters—just for the fun of displaying her power. She laughed at beggars and turned them away from her door.

One day Secretary Chin fell out of his small yellow pleasure boat and sank like a piece of carved jade to the bottom of the lake. That was the end of Secretary Chin, and it was also the end of his wife's idleness and luxury.

"Good Chin Yu Min," said her neighbors, "please allow us to help you in this time of loss."

"Aiyi!" Chin Yu Min scoffed. "I don't need help from such as you. Be off!"

She slammed the door in their faces and stomped away. For many months Chin Yu Min scolded her servants and haggled suspiciously with the merchants. She was sure that everyone was out to cheat her, and she answered their pleasant words with bitter ones.

40

Coin by square-holed coin, her strings of cash flowed away like streams from a fishpond. Chin Yu Min knew she would soon be poor, but she would rather have eaten ashes than let anyone know of this fact.

"Aiyi!" Chin Yu Min screamed at her servants. "You are all less than useless! Leave my house!" When they had gone, she lived alone and tended house with her own hands to save money.

"Esteemed Chin Yu Min," said her neighbors, "allow us to help you."

"Who asked for your help?" Chin Yu Min retorted.

She slammed the door in their faces and stomped away.

41

Chin Yu Min lived alone for several more months, becoming poorer and poorer. At last she was as poor as a mouse in a monastery.

Not one chicken scratched in her yard. Her rice jar stood cracked and empty. The fine lacquer bowls were dulled by hard use, and the lettered scrolls of sheerest paper flapped like ragged ghosts from the walls.

One morning when Chin Yu Min awoke, she knew there was not a thing in the house to eat. She knew there was no cash with which to buy rice.

"I will fish," Chin Yu Min announced to her empty house and the tattered scrolls.

With this decision firmly made, Chin Yu Min took a string and a hairpin for a hook and went to the lake. She stood straight and aloof, arms out, eyes forward, line dangling, and waited—oh, for only a little while—before scowling with impatience.

"There are no fish in this lake!" she complained.

But below the surface of the water many fish indeed shuttled back and forth like monkeys at play in the treetops. Chin Yu Min

shook her fist at
the fish and called
them uncivil names.

Then a melodious
splash caught her ear.

"Aiyi!" Chin Yu Min whispered.

On the next dock sat a fine ginger
cat. He draped his long elegant tail into the
water, and

flick!

Out it came with a fish biting the end. The
cat regarded the fish with a solemn look,
blinked, and then quickly ate every bit, scales,
fins, and all.

"Oh, Peerless Ginger Cat!" said Chin Yu Min.
"Catch a fish for me!"

The ginger cat blinked his eyes. "Certainly, Auntie."

He draped his long elegant tail into the water, and

flick!

Out it came with a fish on the end.

Chin Yu Min picked it up and sniffed deeply. "Steamed with ginger and soy sauce, this will be delicious."

Chin Yu Min hurried back to her house with the fish and put it on to cook. But as the aromatic steam curled up around her gray-haired head, Chin Yu Min began to worry.

"I have a fish today, but what will I have tomorrow?" she asked herself.

She peeked out the window. The ginger cat was still sitting on the dock, meditating on a pair of mandarin ducks who swam in graceful harmony through the reeds.

Chin Yu Min had an idea.

"Oh, Gracious Ginger Cat!" the greedy woman said, joining him on the dock. "My house is large, my bed is soft. Why not come and live with me? There you will be safe from dogs, cool in the summer, and warm in the winter. All I ask is that you continue to catch fish."

"I thank you, Venerable Auntie," said the cat. "I accept your offer. You are truly generous."

Chin Yu Min smiled a thin smile and hurried back to her house.

From that day Chin Yu Min's prosperity returned. Surely, her neighbors agreed, she had found a charm to make fish jump from the lake into her basket, for every day she arrived at the market with a load of glittering, glistening fish. Her neighbors looked on as Chin Yu Min hung new scrolls with the characters of "Wise Decision" and "Good Management" on her door, and admired the new lacquer bowls that she bought from the merchants. Chin Yu Min was prosperous indeed.

45

Every day in the afternoon the ginger
cat sat on the dock and draped his long
elegant tail into the water and
flick!

He pulled out fish after fish until they
were piled up like the mountains of
Guilin. Chin Yu Min rubbed her hands
together and counted her strings of cash.

"Auntie," said the ginger cat one day,
"what would you do if I went away?"

"Aiyi!" gasped Chin Yu Min. "Don't
leave me! How would I eat?"

Chin Yu Min wrung her hands.
She could not bear another plunge into
poverty.

"I will stay, Auntie," replied the ginger cat.

In the evenings of the warm months, Chin
Yu Min sat in front of her door watching the
lake with the ginger cat at her side. From time
to time the sound of his purring broke the
stillness, and Chin Yu Min was content as she
watched the cranes fly overhead.

In the evenings of the cool months, Chin Yu
Min sat in front of a fire in the house watching
the coals with the ginger cat at her side. From

time to time the sound of his purring broke the
stillness, and Chin Yu Min was content as she
watched the embers glow at her feet.

"Auntie," said the ginger cat one day, "what
would you do if I went away?"

"Aiyi!" gasped Chin Yu Min. She hastily
stroked his back. "Don't do that to an old
woman!"

Chin Yu Min wrung her hands. She could
not bear another plunge into solitude.

"I will stay, Auntie," replied the ginger cat.

One day a beggar came to the door.

"Please, Virtuous Lady," he said, "have you an old basket in which I may carry my meager belongings?"

"Pah!" said Chin Yu Min. "Filthy beggar! There, take that ragged thing. It's of no use to me."

So saying, she pointed at a torn and tattered basket that lay discarded in the sun.

"Blessings upon you," the beggar said. He hoisted the basket above his head and limped off to town.

Chin Yu Min cast a thoughtful glance out at the lake. It was time for the ginger cat to start fishing for the day.

"Honorable Ginger Cat!" she called out. "Where are you?"

The answer was wind soughing through the trees.

"Delightful Ginger Cat!" she called again. "Where are you?"

The answer was wavelets lapping the pebbled shore. The ginger cat was nowhere.

"He has left me!" Chin Yu Min cried out.

She stood stricken in the doorway, staring at her fine scrolls. "Wise Decision" and "Good Management" mocked her as they rustled in the breeze.

"No more fish!" Chin Yu Min despaired.

The scrolls rustled again.

"No more prosperity!"

The scrolls shivered.

"No more sitting by the fire!"

The scrolls flapped forlornly.

"No more purring!"

The scrolls fell from their hooks.

"No more fine ginger cat to sit beside me!"

Chin Yu Min tore at her hair. "Wise Decision" and "Good Management" lay in shreds at her feet. In despair Chin Yu Min took up a brush and wrote the characters for "Bottomless Sorrow" on her door.

"Have you seen my ginger cat?" Chin Yu Min asked the neighbors. "Help me find my ginger cat!"

Her neighbors frowned. "When we offered you our help, Chin Yu Min, you scorned us."

"I beseech you," Chin Yu Min said. "Most humbly I ask, have you seen my ginger cat?"

"We have not," her neighbors said, taking pity on her bottomless sorrow. "But we have seen a beggar with an old basket pass this way. Perhaps he knows something."

Chin Yu Min stood as still as a plum tree rooted to the ground. As sure as the sun rose and set, she knew that the ginger cat had been sleeping in the basket. She had given him away.

"Where, oh, where has the beggar gone?" Chin Yu Min asked her neighbors.

"To the market," they replied.

Chin Yu Min ran as fast as her skinny old legs would carry her to the market. There, to her amazement, she found many, many beggars, each with a tattered basket. To her, all beggars looked alike, because she had always been too proud to see their faces.

Now she did not know which one had her basket.

"I beg you," she said to the first, "Venerable Old Monk, allow me to buy your basket."

The beggar bowed once and pulled on his thin gray beard. "For ten cash, madam."

Chin Yu Min gritted her teeth. But her ginger cat was worth more than that in fish. She paid the beggar and snatched the basket: empty.

"I beg you," she said to the next, "Spiritual Old Monk, allow me to buy your basket."

The beggar bowed once and tugged his short stubby beard. "For ten cash, madam."

Chin Yu Min gritted her teeth. But her ginger cat was worth more than that in fish. She paid the beggar and snatched the basket: empty.

"I beg you," she said to the third, "Self-Denying Old Monk, allow me to buy your basket."

Before each beggar she humbled herself and paid for the baskets. Her strings of cash were vanishing like water into sand. The longer she searched for her cat, the more desolate she became.

"For ten cash," said another beggar.

Chin Yu Min pulled at her hair. But all the fish in the Middle Kingdom were not equal to her ginger cat. He was worth far, far more in companionship and warmth.

"Ten cash," said the next.

"Ten cash," said another.

At last she had not one single coin left, and Chin Yu Min was as poor as the beggars—even poorer, for each of them had ten cash, and she had none. But more bitter than the loss of her cash was the loss of her cat.

"Let him not catch another fish!" she cried to heaven. "But still let my friend come back to live with me!"

In tears, Chin Yu Min turned away from the market and trod wearily back to the lake. But before she reached her home, she saw another beggar ahead on the road. This beggar, too, had an old basket.

"Most Scholarly Old Monk," cried the proud Chin Yu Min, "pity an old woman as poor as you! I beg you to give me your basket."

Chin Yu Min knelt in the road and kowtowed with her forehead to the dust. Her heart cried out for the ginger cat.

"Certainly, madam," the beggar said. "If I can take away your bottomless sorrow in this way, I will give you my basket."

So saying, he placed the basket on the ground beside her and hobbled away.

Fear shook Chin Yu Min's hands as she opened the basket. Her breath quaked in her throat.

Inside, curled in sleep, was the ginger cat.

"Oh, Generous Friend!" Chin Yu Min cried. "I have found you again!"

"Good afternoon, Auntie," said the ginger cat, stretching his legs. "Isn't it time to fish?"

For her answer Chin Yu Min hugged the cat to her heart.

"Today I fish for you," she said.

With the cat perched on her shoulder, Chin Yu Min walked back to her home. At the doors of her neighbors, she stopped and bowed.

"Please honor me by taking a meal at my house," she said. "My table is poor, but your presence will make it seem rich to me."

Her neighbors returned her bows and accepted with thanks.

And from that time the scrolls on Chin Yu Min's door read "Contented Joy."

Theme Introduction

Kindness

In this section of the book, you will read about characters who do kind things for others and characters who receive kindness from someone else. Thinking about these stories, and about your own experiences giving and receiving kindness, will give you new ideas about what it means to be kind.

IMPORTANT QUESTIONS TO THINK ABOUT

Before starting this section, think about your own experiences with kindness:

- Can you remember a time when you were kind? When someone was kind to you?

- What kinds of things do people do to show kindness?

Once you have thought about your own experiences with kindness, think about this **theme question** and write down your answers or share them aloud:

What are some reasons that people do kind things?

After reading each story in this section, ask yourself the theme question again. You may have some new ideas you want to add.

What was that shining in the old woman's hand?

THE GOLD COIN

Alma Flor Ada

Juan had been a thief for many years.
Because he did his stealing by night, his skin
had become pale and sickly. Because he spent
his time either hiding or sneaking about, his
body had become shriveled and bent. And
because he had neither friend nor relative to
make him smile, his face was always twisted
into an angry frown.

One night, drawn by a light shining through
the trees, Juan came upon a hut. He crept up
to the door and through a crack saw an old
woman sitting at a plain wooden table.

What was that shining in her hand? Juan
wondered. He could not believe his eyes: it
was a gold coin. Then he heard the woman
say to herself, "I must be the richest person
in the world."

Juan decided instantly that all the woman's
gold must be his. He thought that the easiest
thing to do was to watch until the woman left.
Juan hid in the bushes and huddled under his
poncho, waiting for the right moment to enter
the hut.

Juan was half asleep when he heard
knocking at the door and the sound of insistent
voices. A few minutes later, he saw the woman,
wrapped in a black cloak, leave the hut with
two men at her side.

Here's my chance! Juan
thought. And, forcing open
a window, he climbed
into the empty hut.

He looked about eagerly for the gold. He
looked under the bed. It wasn't there. He
looked in the cupboard. It wasn't there, either.
Where could it be? Close to despair, Juan tore
away some beams supporting the thatch roof.

Finally, he gave up. There was simply no
gold in the hut.

All I can do, he thought, is find the old
woman and make her tell me where she's
hidden it.

So he set out along the path that she and her
two companions had taken.

It was daylight by the time Juan reached
the river. The countryside had been deserted,
but here, along the riverbank, were two huts.
Nearby, a man and his son were hard at work,
hoeing potatoes.

It had been a long, long time since Juan had spoken to another human being. Yet his desire to find the woman was so strong that he went up to the farmers and asked, in a hoarse, raspy voice, "Have you seen a short, gray-haired woman, wearing a black cloak?"

"Oh, you must be looking for Doña Josefa," the young boy said. "Yes, we've seen her. We went to fetch her this morning, because my grandfather had another attack of—"

"Where is she now?" Juan broke in.

"She is long gone," said the father with a smile. "Some people from across the river came looking for her, because someone in their family is sick."

"How can I get across the river?" Juan asked anxiously.

"Only by boat," the boy answered. "We'll row you across later, if you'd like." Then turning back to his work, he added, "But first we must finish digging up the potatoes."

The thief muttered, "Thanks." But he quickly grew impatient. He grabbed a hoe and began to help the pair of farmers. The sooner we finish, the sooner we'll get across the river, he thought. And the sooner I'll get to my gold!

It was dusk when they finally laid down their hoes. The soil had been turned, and the wicker baskets were brimming with potatoes.

"Now can you row me across?" Juan asked the father anxiously.

"Certainly," the man said. "But let's eat supper first."

Juan had forgotten the taste of a home-cooked meal and the pleasure that comes from sharing it with others. As he sopped up the last of the stew with a chunk of dark bread, memories of other meals came back to him from far away and long ago.

By the light of the moon, father and son guided their boat across the river.

"What a wonderful healer Doña Josefa is!" the boy told Juan. "All she had to do to make Abuelo better was give him a cup of her special tea."

"Yes, and not only that," his father added, "she brought him a gold coin."

Juan was stunned. It was one thing for Doña Josefa to go around helping people, but how could she go around handing out gold coins— *his gold coins?*

When the threesome finally reached the other side of the river, they saw a young man sitting outside his hut.

"This fellow is looking for Doña Josefa," the father said, pointing to Juan.

"Oh, she left some time ago," the young man said.

"Where to?" Juan asked tensely.

"Over to the other side of the mountain," the young man replied, pointing to the vague outline of mountains in the night sky.

"How did she get there?" Juan asked, trying to hide his impatience.

"By horse," the young man answered. "They came on horseback to get her because someone had broken his leg."

"Well, then I need a horse, too," Juan said urgently.

"Tomorrow," the young man replied softly. "Perhaps I can take you tomorrow, maybe the next day. First I must finish harvesting the corn."

So Juan spent the next day in the fields, bathed in sweat from sunup to sundown.

Yet each ear of corn that he picked seemed to bring him closer to his treasure. And later that evening, when he helped the young man husk several ears so they could boil them for supper, the yellow kernels glittered like gold coins.

While they were eating, Juan thought about Doña Josefa. Why, he wondered, would someone who said she was the world's richest woman spend her time taking care of every sick person for miles around?

The following day, the two set off at dawn. Juan could not recall when he last had noticed the beauty of the sunrise. He felt strangely moved by the sight of the mountains, barely lit by the faint rays of the morning sun.

As they neared the foothills, the young man said, "I'm not surprised you're looking for Doña Josefa. The whole countryside needs her. I went for her because my wife had been running a high fever. In no time at all, Doña Josefa had her on the road to recovery. And what's more, my friend, she brought her a gold coin!"

Juan groaned inwardly. To think that someone could hand out gold so freely! What a strange woman Doña Josefa is, Juan thought. Not only is she willing to help one person after another, but she doesn't mind traveling all over the countryside to do it!

"Well, my friend," said the young man finally, "this is where I must leave you. But you don't have far to walk. See that house over there? It belongs to the man who broke his leg."

The young man stretched out his hand to say goodbye. Juan stared at it for a moment. It had been a long, long time since the thief had shaken hands with anyone. Slowly, he pulled out a hand from under his poncho. When his companion grasped it firmly in his own, Juan felt suddenly warmed, as if by the rays of the sun.

But after he thanked the young man, Juan ran down the road. He was still eager to catch up with Doña Josefa. When he reached the house, a woman and a child were stepping down from a wagon.

"Have you seen Doña Josefa?" Juan asked.

"We've just taken her to Don Teodosio's," the woman said. "His wife is sick, you know—"

"How do I get there?" Juan broke in. "I've got to see her."

"It's too far to walk," the woman said amiably. "If you'd like, I'll take you there tomorrow. But first I must gather my squash and beans."

So Juan spent yet another long day in the fields. Working beneath the summer sun, Juan noticed that his skin had begun to tan. And although he had to stoop down to pick the squash, he found that he could now stretch his body. His back had begun to straighten, too.

Later, when the little girl took him by the hand to show him a family of rabbits burrowed under a fallen tree, Juan's face broke into a smile. It had been a long, long time since Juan had smiled.

Yet his thoughts kept coming back to the gold.

The following day, the wagon carrying Juan and the woman lumbered along a road lined with coffee fields.

The woman said, "I don't know what we would have done without Doña Josefa. I sent my daughter to our neighbor's house, who then brought Doña Josefa on horseback. She set my husband's leg and then showed me how to brew a special tea to lessen the pain."

Getting no reply, she went on. "And, as if that weren't enough, she brought him a gold coin. Can you imagine such a thing?"

Juan could only sigh. No doubt about it, he thought, Doña Josefa is someone special. But Juan didn't know whether to be happy that Doña Josefa had so much gold she could freely hand it out, or angry for her having already given so much of it away.

69

When they finally reached Don Teodosio's house, Doña Josefa was already gone. But here, too, there was work that needed to be done. . . .

Juan stayed to help with the coffee harvest. As he picked the red berries, he gazed up from time to time at the trees that grew, row upon row, along the hillsides. What a calm, peaceful place this is! he thought.

The next morning, Juan was up at daybreak. Bathed in the soft dawn light, the mountains seemed to smile at him. When Don Teodosio offered him a lift on horseback, Juan found it difficult to have to say goodbye.

"What a good woman Doña Josefa is!" Don Teodosio said, as they rode down the hill toward the sugar cane fields. "The minute she heard about my wife being sick, she came with her special herbs. And as if that weren't enough, she brought my wife a gold coin!"

In the stifling heat, the kind that often signals the approach of a storm, Juan simply sighed and mopped his brow. The pair continued riding for several hours in silence.

Juan then realized he was back in familiar territory, for they were now on the stretch of road he had traveled only a week ago—though how much longer it now seemed to him. He jumped off Don Teodosio's horse and broke into a run.

This time the gold would not escape him! But he had to move quickly, so he could find shelter before the storm broke.

Out of breath, Juan finally reached Doña Josefa's hut. She was standing by the door, shaking her head slowly as she surveyed the ransacked house.

"So I've caught up with you at last!" Juan shouted, startling the old woman. "Where's the gold?"

"The gold coin?" Doña Josefa said, surprised and looking at Juan intently. "Have you come for the gold coin? I've been trying hard to give it to someone who might need it," Doña Josefa said. "First to an old man who had just gotten over a bad attack. Then to a young woman who had been running a fever. Then to a man with a broken leg. And finally to Don Teodosio's wife. But none of them would take it. They all said, 'Keep it. There must be someone who needs it more.'"

Juan did not say a word.

"You must be the one who needs it," Doña Josefa said.

She took the coin out of her pocket and handed it to him. Juan stared at the coin, speechless.

At that moment a young girl appeared, her long braid bouncing as she ran. "Hurry, Doña Josefa, please!" she said breathlessly. "My mother is all alone, and the baby is due any minute."

"Of course, dear," Doña Josefa replied. But as she glanced up at the sky, she saw nothing but black clouds. The storm was nearly upon them. Doña Josefa sighed deeply.

"But how can I leave now? Look at my house! I don't know what has happened to the roof. The storm will wash the whole place away!"

And there was a deep sadness in her voice.

Juan took in the child's frightened eyes, Doña Josefa's sad, distressed face, and the ransacked hut.

"Go ahead, Doña Josefa," he said. "Don't worry about your house. I'll see that the roof is back in shape, good as new."

The woman nodded gratefully, drew her cloak about her shoulders, and took the child by the hand. As she turned to leave, Juan held out his hand.

"Here, take this," he said, giving her the gold coin. "I'm sure the newborn will need it more than I."

There once lived an honest old man.

The Magic Listening Cap

Japanese folktale
as told by Yoshiko Uchida

There once lived an honest old man who was kind and good, but who was so poor, he hardly had enough to eat each day. What made him sadder than not having enough to eat himself was that he could no longer bring an offering to his guardian god at the nearby shrine.

"If only I could bring even an offering of fish," he thought sadly.

Finally, one day, when his house was empty and he had nothing left to eat, he walked to the shrine of his god. He got on his knees and bowed down before him.

"I've come today to offer the only thing I have left," he said sadly. "I have only myself to offer now. Take my life if you will have it."

The old man knelt silently and
waited for the god to speak.

Soon there was a faint rumbling,
and the man heard a voice that
seemed to come from far, far away.

"Don't worry, old man," the god said to
him. "You have been honest and you have
been good. From today on I shall change
your fortune, and you shall suffer no longer."

Then the guardian god gave the old man a
little red cap. "Take this cap, old man," he said.
"It is a magic listening cap. With this on your
head, you will be able to hear such sounds as
you have never heard before."

The old man looked up in surprise. He was old, but he heard quite well, and he had heard many, many sounds during the long years of his life.

"What do you mean?" he asked. "What new sounds are there in this world that I have not yet heard?"

The god smiled. "Have you ever really heard what the nightingale says as it flies to the plum tree in the spring? Have you ever understood what the trees whisper to one another when their leaves rustle in the wind?"

The old man shook his head. He understood.

"Thank you, dear god," he said. "I shall treasure my magic cap forever." And carrying it carefully, he hurried toward his home.

As the old man walked along, the sun grew hot, and he stopped to rest in the shade of a big tree that stood at the roadside. Suddenly, he saw two black crows fly into the tree. One came from the mountains, and the other from the sea. He could hear their noisy chatter fill the air above him. Now was the time to try his magic cap! Quickly, he put it on, and as

soon as he did, he
could understand
everything the crows
were saying.

"And how is life in the
land beyond the sea?"
asked the mountain crow.

"Ah, life is not easy,"
answered the crow of the
sea. "It grows harder and
harder to find food for my
young ones. But tell me, do
you have any interesting
news from the mountains?"

"All is not well in our land either," answered the crow from the mountains. "We are worried about our friend, the camphor tree, who grows weaker and weaker, but can neither live nor die."

"Why, how can that be?" asked the crow of the sea.

"It is an interesting tale," answered the mountain crow. "About six years ago, a wealthy man in our town built a guest house in his garden. He cut down the camphor tree in order to build the house, but the roots were never dug out. The tree is not dead, but neither can it live, for each time it sends new shoots out from beneath the house, they are cut off by the gardener."

"Ah, the poor tree," said the crow of the sea sympathetically. "What will it do?"

"It cries and moans constantly, but alas, human beings are very stupid," said the mountain crow. "No one seems to hear it, and it has cast an evil spell on the wealthy man and made him very ill. If they don't dig up the tree and plant it where it can grow, the spell will not be broken and the man will soon die. He has been ill a long time."

The two crows sat in the tree and talked of many things, but the old man who listened below could not forget the story of the dying man and the camphor tree.

"If only I could save them both," he thought. "I am probably the only human being who knows what is making the man ill."

He got up quickly, and all the way home, he tried to think of some way in which he might save the dying man. "I could go to his home and tell him exactly what I heard," he thought. "But surely no one will believe me if I say I heard two crows talking in a tree. I must think of a clever way to be heard and believed."

As he walked along, a good idea suddenly came to him. "I shall go disguised as a fortune teller," he thought. "Then surely they will believe me."

The very next day the old man took his little red cap, and set out for the town where the sick man lived. He walked by the front gate of this man's home, calling in a loud voice, "Fortunes! Fortunes! I tell fortunes!" Soon the gate flew open and the sick man's wife came rushing out.

"Come in, old man. Come in," she called. "Tell me how I can make my husband well. I have had doctors from near and far, but not one can tell me what to do."

The old man went inside and listened to the woman's story. "We have tried herbs and

82

medicines from many, many lands, but nothing seems to help him," she said sadly.

Then the old man said, "Did you not build a guest house in your garden six years ago?" The wife nodded. "And hasn't your husband been ill ever since?"

"Why, yes," answered the wife, nodding. "That's right. How did you know?"

"A fortune teller knows many things," the old man answered, and then he said, "Let me sleep in your guest house tonight, and by tomorrow I shall be able to tell you how your husband can be cured."

"Yes, of course," the wife answered. "We shall do anything you say."

And so, that night after a sumptuous feast, the old man was taken to the guest house. A beautiful new quilt was laid out for him on the

tatami, and a charcoal brazier was brought
in to keep him warm.

As soon as he was quite alone, the old
man put on his little red cap and sat quietly,
waiting to hear the camphor tree speak. He
slid open the paper doors and looked out
at the sky sprinkled with glowing stars. He
waited and he waited, but the night was
silent and he didn't even hear the whisper
of a sound. As he sat in the darkness, the
old man began to wonder if the crows had
been wrong.

"Perhaps there is no dying camphor tree after all," he thought. And still wearing his red cap, the old man climbed into the quilts and closed his eyes.

Suddenly, he heard a soft rustling sound, like many leaves fluttering in the wind. Then he heard a low gentle voice.

"How do you feel tonight, camphor tree?" the voice called into the silence.

Then the old man heard a hollow sound that seemed to come from beneath the floor.

"Ah, is that you, pine tree?" it asked weakly. "I do not feel well at all. I think I am about to die . . . about to die . . ." it wailed softly.

Soon, another voice whispered, "It's I, the cedar from across the path. Do you feel better tonight, camphor tree?"

And one after the other, the trees of the garden whispered gently to the camphor tree, asking how it felt. Each time, the camphor tree answered weakly, "I am dying . . . I am dying . . ."

The old man knew that if the tree died, the master of the house would also die. Early the next morning, he hurried to the bedside of the dying man. He told him about the tree and about the evil spell it had cast upon him.

"If you want to live," he said, "have the camphor tree dug up quickly, and plant it somewhere in your garden where it can grow."

The sick man nodded weakly. "I will do anything, if only I can become well and strong again."

And so, that very morning, carpenters and gardeners were called to come from the village. The carpenters tore out the floor of the guest house and found the stump of the camphor tree.

Carefully, carefully, the gardeners lifted it out of the earth and then moved it into the garden where it had room to grow. The old man, wearing his red cap, watched as the tree was planted where the moss was green and moist.

"Ah, at last," he heard the camphor tree sigh. "I can reach up again to the good clean air. I can grow once more!"

As soon as the tree was transplanted, the wealthy man began to grow stronger. Before long, he felt so much better he could get up for a few hours each day. Then he was up all day long, and, finally, he was completely well.

"I must thank the old fortune teller for saving my life," he said, "for if he had not come to tell me about the camphor tree, I would probably not be alive today."

And so he sent for the old man with the little red cap.

"You were far wiser than any of the doctors who came from near and far to see me," he said to the old man. Then, giving him many

bags filled with gold, he said, "Take this gift,
and with it my lifelong thanks. And when this
gold is gone, I shall see that you get more."

"Ah, you are indeed very kind," the old man
said happily, and taking his gold, he set off for
home.

As soon as he got home, he took some
of the gold coins and went to the village
market. There he bought rice cakes and sweet

tangerines and the very best fish he could find. He hurried with them to his guardian god, and placed them before his shrine.

"My fortunes have indeed changed since you gave me this wonderful magic cap," the old man said. "I thank you more than I can say."

Each day after that, the old man went to the shrine, and never forgot to bring an offering of rice or wine or fish to his god. He was able to live in comfort, and never had to worry again about not having enough to eat. And, because he was not a greedy man, he put away his magic listening cap and didn't try to tell any more fortunes. Instead, he lived quietly and happily the rest of his days.

"You can trust me."

THE MUSHROOM MAN

Ethel Pochocki

There once was a man who spent his days in the dark. He worked in a mushroom farm, a long, low, windowless building where mushrooms grew in beds of black soil, and everything had the earthy smell of mold.

The man rarely saw the sun, except in the summer when it rose with him, or when it streaked scarlet-purple across the sky as he walked home after work.

When the people of the town saw him on the street, they snickered at his strange appearance. They called him the mushroom man, for indeed he did resemble the crop he tended. His round, oversized head was a bit too large for the rest of his body, and his flesh, pale as paste, was spongy to the touch. His deeply set eyes blinked often, and he walked slightly bent over, with soft shuffling steps.

Children would follow him, at a safe distance, and chant in their high singsong voices:

Watch out for the mushroom man,
The mushroom man, the mushroom man,
He'll eat you up in a frying pan,
Fast as he can, fast as he can!

Then their parents would call to them and tell them to stop that right now and come home, and they would run off laughing.

The mushroom man never answered them. He just kept on walking as if he did not hear. He knew he could not change their minds. They had already judged him by his appearance. They seemed to fear that they, too, might turn into mushroom people if they got too close to him.

The mushroom man accepted this without resentment, for he had been blessed with a cheerful disposition.

For the most part, he was quite content.
Still there was this little ache now and then,
sometimes dull, as in old bones on a rainy day,
sometimes sharp as a wasp sting. Sometimes
it came when he was most content, because
he had no one with whom to share his good
feelings.

He knew the ache was loneliness, and he
learned to live with it, as one would with a
grouchy relative. "After all," he said to himself,
"nothing's perfect."

He was comfortable living in the little
basement room of an apartment house. When

he got home, he would open a can of vegetable soup and a box of crackers and eat his dinner in the big brown overstuffed chair that made him itch, and he would listen to the news on the radio or to the ticking of his wind-up clock.

Sometimes when the weather allowed, he would make a sandwich, stick it into his pocket, and go down to the riverbank in the park. There he would sit on a bench and eat his peanut butter and marshmallow fluff sandwich, watching the strolling people and playful squirrels.

He found comfort in the antics of the squirrels. They chattered in front of him without fear. He would sometimes offer them bits of his sandwich, which they would politely decline.

As he watched them, an idea began to grow in his mind. Perhaps he might share his life with a pet. A pet would be his friend, one who would like him just as he was. He knew it would not be a squirrel—they were too nervous to listen to poetry—or a dog. He did not like dogs. He supposed there might be some good ones somewhere, but he had been chased by too many whose snarling teeth had nearly nabbed him. No, it would not be a dog.

Suddenly the squirrels scurried, as a cat walked up the path toward the mushroom man. A creamy white creature with a superior air, she ambled past, ignoring him, then stopped to nab a flea on her rump. After disposing of it, she sat in the middle of the path, cleaning her ears as if it were her private dressing room.

The mushroom man could not take his eyes off her. What a delightful creature! What exquisite coloring!

The cat looked straight at him, walked over, jumped into his lap, and put her paws on his chest. He noticed that she was slightly cross-eyed, but that only added to her charm.

He stroked her white fur and rubbed her ears.

"Do you have a home, pretty one?" he asked.

"No," she purred.

"Would you like to come with me? I have sardines in the can."

"Yes," she purred even louder and licked his nose.

And so they left the park together and returned to his apartment. That night, as he settled into bed, the cat hugging his feet, he thought, "Now I am a completely happy man!"

He named the cat Beatrice, and she became absolute mistress of his home. While he worked, he thought of little else but coming home and spending the evening with Beatrice, watching her enchanting tricks and listening to her vast collection of songs.

Beatrice enjoyed the attention, the adoration, the chicken livers, the satin pillow—but after a while, she grew weary of it. Oh, the man was kind in a dull sort of way, but she was beginning to tire of being locked up and treated like a delicate toy. At heart, she was not one who could be satisfied with hearth and home.

"I was born to wander," she sighed plaintively as she sat before the mirror, pluming her tail like a peacock. She decided it would be best for both of them if she left before the mushroom man became too attached.

And so one starry night as they sat on the bench in the park and he began explaining to her the position of Venus in the autumn sky, she quietly disappeared into a clump of yew bushes.

The mushroom man searched, calling out to her, pleading for her return, but Beatrice never came back. He sat on the bench, sighing sadly. Perhaps it was his fate to be alone.

The earth beneath his feet began to move.
Something was making a tunnel. Then more
tunnels spread out, crisscrossing each other
like sled tracks in the snow. The plowing
stopped. A small black-furred animal with a
long, narrow nose burst from a tunnel and
appeared to be checking out his workmanship.

"Helloo—" said the mushroom man softly,
so as not to startle the creature. The animal
dashed back into the hole, almost missing it in
his panic.

"Please come back," cried the man, "I won't
hurt you! We could enjoy the evening together.
I just want to be friendly."

After a short silence, a muffled response came from the tunnel. "We can talk, but I'll stay down here, thank you."

"Oh, please come out," pleaded the mushroom man, "whoever you are! It's such a lovely night. Don't you love the moonlight? I much prefer it to the sun."

A furry head appeared, slowly, cautiously. "I'm a mole, and I'll stay right here, thank you. You have a kind voice, but I can't afford to go around trusting anyone. You could be waiting to trick me with a trap or poison."

"You can trust *me*," said the mushroom man. "I said I won't hurt you, and I'm a man of my word. You can sit over there by that clump of irises. I couldn't reach you if I tried. Come, share the moonlight."

"Don't you know anything about moles?" asked the animal in weary exasperation. "Moles are blind. We can't see the moonlight or irises or anything."

"Oh, I *am* sorry," said the mushroom man, embarrassed. "I didn't realize—please forgive me."

The mole emerged from the hole completely. "Nothing to forgive," he said a bit too cheerfully. "That's just the way things are, and we do quite well, thank you, without sight. No point in making a fuss."

"I admire your spunk and courage," said the mushroom man.

"Well," said the mole, his voice quivering slightly, "I can stand being in the dark, but it's being alone that's difficult. I lost most of my family in a flood—I escaped when I was thrown headfirst into a drainpipe. The others were caught in a trap and made into a muff."

"I'm so sorry," the mushroom man said again. "I—I am quite alone myself. As for the dark, I'm rather fond of it. I think there's much to be said for being in the dark. Would you believe that I even work in the dark all day?"

"No, go on!" said the mole, wiping away the few tears that had escaped when he spoke of his lost family.

The mushroom man told him about the farm and how he picked and packed the pearly beauties by the light of his headlamp.

"Do you like mushrooms?" he asked the mole.

The mole laughed, lightly at first, and then with such gusto he began to roll around in a patch of wild peppermint.

"What's so funny?" asked the mushroom man.

"*Do I like mushrooms?* My friend, mushrooms are right up there with worms and grubs! I could show you mushrooms you wouldn't believe. Right *now*—what do you say, are you up for adventure?"

"Of course!" cried the mushroom man, almost dancing at the thought of a shared adventure.

Off they went lickety-split into the deep woods. Even though he was blind, the mole was swift and sure of the path. The

mushroom man could barely keep up with him. They came to an oak tree on a small hill, and the mole began to sniff and dig into the side of it. In a few moments, he came up with something dark and squishy in the shape of a flattened ear.

"Truffles!" exclaimed the mushroom man. "The rarest and most delicious of all mushrooms! I haven't had a truffle in ages. I shall cook it up with a bit of butter and a dash of wine. Will you do me the honor of sharing this delicacy?"

The mole did not answer. He remembered his unfortunate relatives made into a muff. Could he trust a human?

"It has been a long time since I have had a dinner guest," the mushroom man said softly. "We could tell riddles and write poems, and you could tell me about life beneath the earth. Do you like apple crisp?"

The mole decided to risk all. "Of course I will come. How kind of you to invite me," he said, knowing he had sealed his fate, for better or worse. And off they went, without further talk.

After dinner, which each assured the other
was the most scrumptious ever, they ate
yogurt-covered raisins and toasted their feet by
the artificial fire. (The mole, never having seen
a real fireplace, said the crackling sounded
quite real to him.) They talked of many things
and found they were in agreement about
most of them, and then they said good night,
promising to meet the next evening for dinner.

And so they did, and for every evening
thereafter, until the trees were bare of leaves.
With the first frost, the mushroom man invited
the mole to spend the winter with him, and the
mole accepted. The mushroom man brought
a basket of dirt from the mushroom farm and
set it up in the cool pantry, so the mole could
burrow himself a bed.

During the day, the mole tended to the
house—washed the dishes, shook out the rugs,
made lentil soup and banana fritters—because
he was very smart and remembered where
everything was.

When Christmas arrived, they trimmed a
small fir tree with cranberries and dried apple
rings, nibbling as they worked. The mole gave
the mushroom man a pair of sunglasses with
sparkly red rims, a vanilla bean, and a poem
he wrote about moon shadows dancing on the
snow, as he imagined them. (The mushroom
man framed it the day after Christmas and
hung it above the fireplace.)

The mushroom man gave the mole a tin
of worms imported from France, two pairs of
green wool slipper socks (one pair for the front

paws, one for the back), and a music box that played "You Are My Sunshine."

Each declared his gifts exactly what he most wanted, but they agreed, as they sat before the fire sipping spiced cider, that the very best gift of all was having a friend.

Theme Introduction

Confidence

In this book, you will read about characters who learn to feel sure of themselves, even in tough situations. Thinking about these stories, and about your own experiences, will give you new ideas about what it means to be confident.

IMPORTANT QUESTIONS TO THINK ABOUT

Before starting this book, think about times you felt confident or struggled to feel confident:

• Can you think of a time when you felt very sure of yourself?

• What do you do to help yourself feel confident when you are scared or nervous?

Once you have thought about your own experiences with confidence, think about this **theme question** and write down your answers or share them aloud:

How does someone become confident?

After reading each story in this section, ask yourself the theme question again. You may have some new ideas you want to add.

"One day the heart and banza will be one."

THE BANZA

Haitian folktale
as told by Diane Wolkstein

On the island of Haiti there once lived a little tiger named Teegra and a little goat named Cabree. Usually tigers and goats are enemies, but these two were best friends.

They had met during a thunderstorm when they had each run into the same cave for shelter. The storm had lasted all night, and when they came out in the morning, everything seemed strange to them, for they had come out of the cave by a different entrance and were lost.

They were both quite small, lonely, and afraid.

They looked at each other.

Cabree brayed, "Be-be. . . ."

Teegra roared, "Rrr. . . ."

"Do you want to be friends?" Cabree asked.

"Now!" Teegra answered.

So they wandered over the countryside, playing together, sharing whatever food they found, and sleeping close to each other at night for warmth.

Then one morning, they found themselves in front of the cave where they had first met.

"rrRRRRR!"

Cabree turned. But it was not Teegra who had roared.

"RRRRRRrrr-rrRR!"

It was a roar of another tiger.

"Mama! Papa! *Auntie!*" Teegra cried joyfully as three huge tigers bounded out of the bushes.

Cabree ran into the cave without waiting.

After a while, Teegra went to find Cabree, but Cabree refused to come out of the cave, so Teegra went home with his family.

The next morning, Teegra went to the cave alone.

"Cabree!" he called. "I brought you a banza."

Cabree poked her head out of the cave.

"A *ban-za*? What's that?"

"A little banjo," Teegra said. "It belonged to my uncle, but I want you to have it—so it will protect you."

"How will the banza protect me?" Cabree asked.

"Auntie says, 'The banza belongs to the heart, and there is no stronger protection than the heart.' When you play the banza, Auntie says to place it over your heart, and 'one day the heart and banza will be one.' "

"Is that true?"

"Oh, Cabree, I don't really know, but I know I shall not forget you."

Teegra placed the banza around his friend's neck, then he turned to go.

"Where are you going?" Cabree asked.

"Home!" Teegra answered, and the little tiger ran back to his family without stopping.

Cabree stepped out of the cave so she
could see the banza more clearly. It was a
beautiful banza, and when the sun shone on
it, it gleamed. Cabree held the banza over her
heart. She stroked it gently. A friendly,
happy sound came out. She stroked it
again—and again—and before she
realized it, she was trotting through
the forest, humming to herself and
stopping now and then to play a
tune on the banza.

One afternoon Cabree came to a spring. She wanted to drink, but she was afraid the banza would get wet, so she took it off and carefully laid it down in the bushes. As she drank the cool sweet water, she heard a low growl behind her.

"rrrRRrrr. . . ."

Turning quickly, Cabree saw four large hungry tigers. Cabree wanted to leap across the stream and run away, but the banza was in the bushes behind the tigers. No! She would not leave the banza Teegra had given her.

Slowly and fiercely Cabree walked toward
the banza.

Another tiger appeared. Now there were five.

Cabree kept walking.

"Where are you going?" the leader shouted.

Cabree reached the bushes. She picked
up the banza and hung it around her
neck. Then she turned to the tigers.
Five more jumped out of the bushes.

Now there were ten!

"What have you put around your neck?"
asked the leader.

And Cabree, trying to quiet her thundering,
pounding heart, brought her foreleg to her chest
and, by mistake, plucked the banza.

"A musician!" said the chief, laughing. "So
you wish to play us a song?"

"No!" said Cabree.

"No?" echoed the leader. And all the tigers
took a step closer to Cabree.

Teegra! Cabree wanted to shout. But Teegra
was far away, and she was alone, surrounded by
the tigers. No, she was not completely alone. She
still had the banza Teegra had given her.

Cabree's heart beat very fast, but in time
to her heartbeat, she stroked the banza. She
opened her mouth, and a song came out. To her
own surprise, it was a loud, low, ferocious song:

Ten fat tigers, ten fat tigers,
Cabree eats tigers raw.
Yesterday Cabree ate ten tigers;
Today Cabree eats ten more.

The tigers were astonished.

"Who is Cabree? And where did you learn that song?" demanded the chief.

"I am Cabree." Cabree answered in a new deep voice, and noticing how frightened the tigers looked, she added, "And that is *my* song. I always sing it before dinner."

The tiger chief realized that three of his tigers had suddenly disappeared.

"Madame Cabree," he said, "you play beautifully. Permit me to offer you a drink."

"Very well," said Cabree.

"Bring Madame Cabree a drink!" he ordered the two tigers closest to him, and as they started to leave he whispered, "and don't come back."

Five tigers stared at Madame Cabree.

Cabree stared back. Then she stroked her banza and sang, a little slower, but just as intently:

Five fat tigers, five fat tigers,
Cabree eats tigers raw.
Yesterday Cabree ate ten tigers;
Today Cabree eats five more.

"Oh! Oh-h-h! Something dreadful must have happened to my tigers," said the leader. "You." He motioned to the two tigers nearest him. "Go fetch Madame Cabree a drink." And again he whispered, "And don't come back."

Now only three tigers quaked before Madame Cabree. Cabree sang again:

Three fat tigers, three fat tigers,
Cabree eats tigers raw.
Yesterday Cabree ate ten tigers;
Today Cabree eats three more.

When she finished her song, only the leader remained. Cabree began:

One fat tiger—

"Please," whispered
the leader, "please let me
go. I promise no tiger will
ever bother you again."
Cabree looked at the
trembling tiger. All she had
done was to play the banza
and sing what was in her
heart. So Teegra's auntie
was right. Her heart had
protected her. Her heart
and her banza.

"Please!" begged
the leader. "I'll do
whatever you wish."
"Then go at once
to Teegra, the little
tiger who lives near the
cave. Tell Teegra: 'Today
Cabree's heart and the banza
are one.'"
"Yes, yes," said the tiger. "Today
Cabree's heart and the banza are
one." And the tiger chief ran off to
find Teegra.

With her banza gleaming around her neck, Cabree went trotting through the forest. But every now and then, she would stop. She would stroke her banza and sing, for her heart would have a new song.

· *Everyone plays, and I am alone.* ·

THE UPSIDE-DOWN BOY

Juan Felipe Herrera

Mama, who loves words, sings out the name
   on the
street sign—Juniper. "Who-nee-purr! Who-nee-purr!"

Papi parks our old army truck on Juniper Street
in front of Mrs. Andasola's tiny pink house.
"We found it at last," Papi shouts, "Who-nee-purr!"

"Time to start school," Mama tells me with music in
   her voice.
"My Who-nee-purr Street!" I yell to the chickens in
   the yard.

125

"Don't worry, *chico*,"
Papi says as he walks me to school.
"Everything changes. A new place has new leaves
on the trees and blows fresh air into your body."

I pinch my ear. Am I really here?
Maybe the street lamp is really a golden cornstalk
with a dusty gray coat.

People speed by alone in their fancy melting cars.
In the valleys, *campesinos* sang "*Buenos días*,
    Juanito."

I make a clown face, half funny,
half scared. "I don't speak English," I say to Papi.
"Will my tongue turn into a rock?"

I slow step into school.
My *burrito de papas*, my potato burrito, in a
    brown bag.
Empty playground,
fences locked. One cloud up high.

No one
in the halls. Open a door with a blue number 27.
"¿Dónde estoy?" Where am I?
My question in Spanish fades
as the thick door slams behind me.

Mrs. Sampson, the teacher, shows me my desk.
Kids laugh when I poke my nose into
   my lunch bag.

The hard round clock above my head
clicks and aims its strange
arrows at me.

On the chalkboard, I see a row
of alphabet letters and addition numbers. If I
    learn them,
will they grow like seeds?

If I learn the English words,
will my voice reach the ceiling, weave through it
    like grapevines?

We are finger-painting.
I make wild suns with my open hands.
Crazy tomato cars and cucumber sombreros—
I write my name with seven chiles.

"What is that?" Mrs. Sampson asks.
My tongue is a rock.

The school bell rings
and shakes me.

I run and grab my lunch bag
   and sit on the green steel bench.
In a few fast minutes, I finish my potato burrito.
But everyone plays,
and I am alone.

"It is only recess,"
my classmate Amanda says in Spanish.
In Spanish, I pronounce "recess" slowly.
"Sounds like *reses*—like the word for cattle,
huh?" I say.

"What is recess?" I ask Amanda.

The high bell
roars again.

This time everyone eats their sandwiches,
while I play in the breezy baseball diamond
by myself.

"Is this recess?" I ask again.

When I jump up,
everyone sits.
When I sit,
all the kids swing through the air.

My feet float through the clouds,
when all I want is to touch the earth.
I am the upside-down boy.

Papi comes home to Mrs. Andasola's pink house.
I show him my finger painting.
"What a spicy sun," he sings out.
"It reminds me of hot summer days in the
    San Joaquin Valley,"
he says, brushing his dark hair with his hands.

"Look, Mama!
See my painting?"

"Those are flying tomatoes
ready for salsa," Mama sings.
She shows my painting to Mrs. Andasola,
who shows it to Gabino, her canary.

"Gabino, Gabino, see?" Mrs. Andasola yells.
"What do you think?"
Gabino nods his head back and forth.
"Pío, pío, piiiii!"

131

Mrs. Sampson invites me
to the front of the class.
    "Sing, Juanito,
sing a song we have been
        practicing."

I pop up shaking. I am
    alone facing the class.

"Ready to sing?" Mrs. Sampson
    asks me.
I am frozen, then a deep
    breath fills me,
"Three blind mice, three
    blind mice," I sing.

My eyes open as big as the ceiling, and
my hands spread out as if catching
raindrops from the sky.

"You have a very beautiful voice, Juanito,"
    Mrs. Sampson says.
"What is beautiful?" I ask Amanda after school.

At home, I help Mama and Mrs. Andasola
make *buñuelos*—fried sweet cinnamon tortilla chips.

"Piiiiicho, come heeeere," I sing out,
calling my dog as I stretch a dough ball.

"Listen to meeeee," I sing to Picho with his ears
curled up into fuzzy triangles. "My voice is
    beauuuuutiful!"

"What is he singing?" Mrs. Andasola asks my mom,
as she gently lays a *buñuelo* into the frying pan.

"My teacher says my voice is beauuuuutiful," I sing,
dancing with a tiny dough ball stuck on my nose.

"*Sí, sí,*" Mama laughs.
"Let's see if your *buñuelos* come out beautiful, too."

133

"I only made it to the third grade, Juanito,"
Mama tells me as I get ready for bed.

"When we lived in El Paso, Texas,
my mother needed help at home. We were
   very poor
and she was tired from cleaning people's houses."

"That year your mama won a spelling medal,"
Papi says as he shaves in the bathroom.

"Your Papi learned English without a school,"
   Mama says.
"When he worked the railroads, he would pay
his buddies a penny for each word they taught him."

Papi says softly, "Each word,
each language has its own magic."

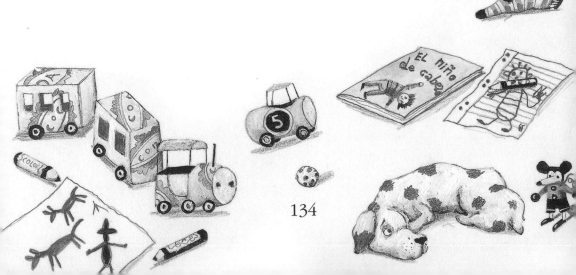

After a week of reading a new poem aloud to
   us every day,
Mrs. Sampson says, "Write a poem,"
as she plays symphony music on the old red
   phonograph.

I think of Mama, squeeze my pencil,
pour letters from the shiny tip like a skinny river.

The waves tumble onto the page.
*L*s curl at the bottom.
*F*s tip their hats from their heads.
*M*s are sea waves. They crash over my table.

• JUAN FELIPE HERRERA •

JUANITO'S POEM

Papi Felipe with a mustache of words.
Mama Lucha with strawberries in her hair.
I see magic salsa in my house
and everywhere!

"I got an A on my poem!" I yell to everyone
in the front yard where Mama gives Papi a
      haircut.

I show Gabino my paper
as I fly through the kitchen to the backyard.

"Listen," I sing to the baby chicks,
with my hands up as if I am a famous music
      conductor.

I sprinkle corn kernels and sing out my poem.
Each fuzzy chick gets a name:
"Beethoven! You are the one with the bushy head!
Mozart! You jumpy black-spotted hen!
Johann Sebastian! Tiny red rooster, dance, dance!"

137

In the morning, as we walk to school,
Papi turns and says, "You do have a nice voice,
    Juanito.
I never heard you sing until yesterday
when you fed the chickens.
At first, when we moved here,
you looked sad, and I didn't know what to do."

"I felt funny, upside down," I say to him.
"The city streets aren't soft with flowers.
Buildings don't have faces. You know, Papi,
in the *campo* I knew all the names, even of
    those bugs
with little wild eyes and shiny noses!"

"Here," he says. "Here's my harmonica.
It has many voices, many beautiful songs
just like you. Sing them!"

On Open House Day,
Mama and Papi sit in the front row.
Mrs. Andasola admires our drawings on the walls,
Gabino on her shoulder.

"Our paintings look like the flowery fields back
in the Valley," I tell Amanda.

"I have a surprise," I whisper to Mama.
"I am *El Maestro* Juanito, the choir conductor!"
Mrs. Sampson smiles wearing a chile sombrero
and puts on the music.

I blow a C with my harmonica—"La la la laaaaah!
Ready to sing out your poems?" I ask my choir.
"*Uno . . . dos . . .* and three!"

"Do you imagine this is the whole of the world?"

THE UGLY DUCKLING

Hans Christian Andersen

It was so lovely in the country—it was summer! The wheat was yellow, the oats were green, the hay was stacked in the green meadows, and down there the stork went tiptoeing on his red legs, jabbering Egyptian, a language his mother had taught him. Round about the fields and meadows were great forests, and in the midst of those forests lay deep lakes. Yes, it was indeed lovely in the country! Bathed in sunshine there stood an old manor house, surrounded by a deep moat, and from the walls down to the water's edge the bank was covered with great wild rhubarb leaves so high that little children could stand

upright under the biggest of them. The place
was as much of a wilderness as the densest
wood, and there sat a duck on her nest; she
was busy hatching her ducklings, but she was
almost tired of it, because sitting is such a
tedious business, and she had very few callers.
The other ducks thought it more fun to swim
about in the moat than to come and have a
gossip with her under a wild rhubarb leaf.

   At last one eggshell after another began to
crack open. "Cheep, cheep!" All the yolks had
come to life and were sticking out their heads.

   "Quack, quack," said the duck, and all her
ducklings came scurrying out as fast as
they could, looking about under
the green leaves, and their
mother let them look as much
as they liked, because
green is good
for the eyes.

"How big the world is!" said all the ducklings, for they felt much more comfortable now than when they were lying in the egg.

"Do you imagine this is the whole of the world?" asked their mother. "It goes far beyond the other side of the garden, right into the Rector's field, but I've never been there yet. I hope you're all here," she went on, and hoisted herself up. "No, I haven't got all of you even now; the biggest egg is still there. I wonder how much longer it will take! I'm getting rather bored with the whole thing." And she squatted down again on the nest.

"Well, how are you getting on?" asked an old duck who came to call on her.

"That last egg is taking an awfully long time," said the brooding duck. "It won't break; but let me show you the others, they're the sweetest ducklings I've ever seen. They are all exactly like their father; the scamp—he never comes to see me!"

"Let me look at the egg that won't break," said the old duck. "You may be sure it's a turkey's egg. I was fooled like that once, and the trouble and bother I had with those youngsters, because

143

they were actually afraid of the water! I simply couldn't get them to go in! I quacked at them and I snapped at them, but it was no use. Let me see the egg—of course it's a turkey's egg. Leave it alone, and teach the other children to swim."

"Oh, well, if I've taken so much trouble I may just as well sit a little longer," said the duck.

"Please yourself," said the old duck, and she waddled off.

At last the big egg cracked. "Cheep, cheep!" said the youngster, scrambling out; he was so big and ugly! The duck looked at him: "What a frightfully big duckling that one is," she said. "None of the others looked like that! Could he possibly be a turkey chick? We'll soon find out; he'll have to go into the water, even if I have to kick him in myself!"

The next day the weather was simply glorious; the sun shone on all the wild rhubarb plants. Mother Duck appeared with her family down by the moat. Splash! There she was in the water! "Quack, quack," she said, and one duckling after another plumped in. The water closed over their heads, but they were up again in a second and floated beautifully. Their legs worked of their own accord; they were all out in the water now, and even the ugly gray creature was swimming along with them.

"That's no turkey!" she said. "Look how nicely he uses his legs, and how straight he holds himself! He's my own flesh and blood, I tell you. He isn't really so bad when you take a good look at him. Quack, quack—come along with me, I'll bring you out into the world and introduce you to the duck yard, but keep close to me or you may get stepped on, and look out for the cat!"

So they made their entrance into the duck yard. What a pandemonium there was! Two families were quarreling over an eel's head; but in the end the cat got it.

"There you are, that's the way of the world!" said Mother Duck, licking her lips, for she did so want the eel's head herself. "Now use your legs," she said. "Move about briskly and curtsey with your necks to the old duck over there; she is the most aristocratic person here, and of Spanish blood, that's why she is so stout; and be sure to observe that red rag round her leg. It's a great distinction, and the highest honor that can be bestowed upon a duck: it means that her owner wishes to keep her, and that she is to be specially noticed by man and beast. Now hurry! Don't turn your toes in; a well-brought-up duckling turns his toes out just as father and mother do—like that. That's right! Now make a deep curtsey with your necks and say, 'Quack, quack!' "

And they did as they were told; but the other ducks all round about looked at them and said out loud, "There now! Have we got to have that crowd too? As if there weren't enough of us already; and ugh, what a dreadful-looking creature that duckling is! We won't put up with him." And immediately a duck rushed at him and bit him in the neck.

"Leave him alone," said the mother. "He's not bothering any of you."

"I know," said the duck who had bitten him, "but he's too big and odd. What he wants is a good smacking."

"Those are pretty children you've got, Mother," said the old duck with the rag round her leg. "They are all nice-looking except that one—he didn't turn out so well. I  wish he could be made all over again!"

"That can't be done, Your Grace," said Mother Duck. "He's not handsome, but he's as good as gold, and he swims as well as any of the others, I daresay even a little better. I expect his looks will improve, or perhaps in time his size won't be so noticeable. He was in the egg too long, that's why he isn't properly shaped." And she pecked his neck and brushed up the little man. "As it happens he's a drake," she added, "so it doesn't matter quite so much. I think he'll be a strong fellow, and I'm sure he'll make his mark in the world."

"The other ducklings are lovely," said the old duck. "Make yourselves at home, and if you find an eel's head—you may bring it to me."

So at once they felt at home.

But the poor duckling who was the last to be hatched, and who looked so ugly, was bitten and buffeted about and made fun of both by the ducks and the hens. "He's too big!" they all said. And the turkey-cock, who was born with spurs and consequently thought he was an emperor, blew himself up like a ship in full sail and made for him, gobbling and gabbling till his wattles were quite purple. The poor duckling did not know where to turn; he was so miserable because of his ugliness, and because he was the butt of the whole barnyard. And so it went on all the first day, and after that matters grew worse and worse. The poor duckling was chased about by everyone; his own brothers and sisters were downright nasty to him and always said, "I hope the cat gets you, you skinny bag of bones!" And even his mother said, "I wish you were miles away!" And the ducks bit him and the hens pecked him, and the girl who fed them kicked him with her foot.

So, half running and half flying, he got over the fence.

The little birds in the bushes rose up in alarm. "That's because I'm so ugly," thought the duckling, and closed his eyes, but he kept on running and finally came out into the great marsh where the wild ducks lived. There he lay the whole night long, tired and downhearted.

In the morning the wild ducks flew up and looked at their new companion. "What sort of a fellow are you?" they asked, and the duckling turned in all directions, bowing to everybody as nicely as he could.

"You're appallingly ugly!" said the wild ducks. "But why should we care so long as you don't marry into our family?"

149

Poor thing! As if he had
any thought of marrying!
All he wanted to do was to
lie among the reeds and
drink a little marsh water.

So he lay there for two
whole days, and then
came two wild geese,
or rather ganders, for they
were two young men;
they had not been out of
the egg very long, and that
was why they were so cocky.

"Listen, young fellow," they
said. "You're so ugly that we
quite like you. Will you join us
and be a bird of passage? Close by,
in another marsh, there are some lovely
wild geese, all nice young girls, and they can
all say 'Quack.' You're so ugly that you might
appeal to them."

Two shots rang out—bang! bang!—both
ganders fell dead among the reeds, and the
water was reddened with their blood. Bang!
bang! was heard again, and whole flocks of

wild geese flew up from the reeds, and—bang!
bang! bang! again and again. A great shoot was
going on. The men were lying under cover
all round the marsh, and some of them were
even up in the trees whose branches stretched
out above the reeds. Blue smoke drifted in
among the dark trees and was carried far
out over the water. Through the mud came
the gun-dogs—splash! splash!—bending
down the reeds and rushes on every
side. The poor duckling was scared
out of his wits, and tried to hide his
head under his wing, when suddenly
a fierce-looking dog came close to
him, with his tongue hanging far
out of his mouth and his wild eyes
gleaming horribly. He opened his
jaws wide, showed his sharp teeth,
and—splash! splash!—off he went
without touching the duckling.

"Thank heaven!" he sighed. "I'm so ugly that
even the dog won't bother to bite me!"

And so he lay perfectly still, while the shots
rattled through the reeds as gun after gun was
fired.

It was toward evening when everything
quieted down, but the poor duckling dared not
stir yet. He waited several hours before he
looked about him, and then hurried away from
the marsh as fast as he could. He ran over field
and meadow, hardly able to fight against
the strong wind.

Late that night he reached
a wretched little hut, so
wretched, in fact, that
it did not know which
way to fall, and that
is why it remained
standing upright. The
wind whistled so fiercely round
the duckling that the poor thing simply had to sit
down on his little tail to resist it.

The storm grew worse and worse. Then he
noticed that the door had come off one of its
hinges and hung so crooked that he could slip
into the room through the opening, and that is
what he did.

An old woman lived here with her tomcat
and her hen. The cat, whom she called "Sonny,"
knew how to arch his back and purr; in fact he

could even give out sparks, but for that you
had to rub his fur the wrong way. The hen
had little short legs and was called "Stumpy."
She was an excellent layer and the old woman
loved her as her own child.

Next morning they at once noticed the
strange duckling; the cat began to purr and
the hen to cluck.

"What's the matter?" asked the old
woman, looking about her; but her eyes
were not very good, and so she mistook
the duckling for a fat duck that had lost
her way. "What a windfall!" she said. "Now
I shall have duck's eggs—if it doesn't happen
to be a drake. We must make sure of that."
So the duckling was taken on trial for three
weeks, but not a single egg came along.

Now the cat was master of the house,
and the hen was mistress, and they always
said, "We, and the world"; for they imagined
themselves to be not only half the world, but
by far the better half. The duckling thought
that other people might be allowed to have
an opinion too, but the hen could not see that
at all.

"Can you lay eggs?" she asked.

"No."

"Well, then, you'd better keep your mouth shut!"

And the cat said, "Can you arch your back, purr, and give out sparks?"

"No."

"Well, then, you can't have any opinion worth offering when sensible people are speaking."

The duckling sat in a corner, feeling very gloomy and depressed. Then he suddenly thought of the fresh air and the bright sunshine, and such a longing came over him to swim in the water that he could not help telling the hen about it.

"What's the matter with you?" asked the hen. "You haven't got anything to do, that's why you get these silly ideas. Either lay eggs or purr and you'll soon be all right."

"But it's so delightful to swim in the water," said the duckling, "so delightful to get it over your head and dive down to the bottom!"

"Yes, it must be delightful!" said the hen. "You've gone crazy, I think. Ask the cat, the cleverest creature I know, if he likes swimming or diving. I say nothing of myself. Ask our mistress, the old woman, as well; no one in the world is wiser than she. Do you think she would like to swim or to get the water over her head?"

"You don't understand me," said the duckling.

"Well, if we don't understand you, then who would? You surely don't imagine you're wiser than the cat or the old woman?—not to mention myself, of course. Don't give yourself such airs, child, but be grateful to your Maker for all the kindness you have received. Didn't you get into a warm room, and haven't you fallen in with people who can teach you a thing or two? But you talk such nonsense, it's no fun at all to have you about. Believe me, I wish you well. I tell you unpleasant things, but that's the way to know one's real friends. Come on, hurry up, see that you lay eggs, and do learn how to purr or to give out sparks!"

"I think I had better go out into the wide world," said the duckling.

"Please yourself," said the hen.

So the duckling went away: he swam in the water and dived down into it, but he was still snubbed by every creature because of his ugliness.

Autumn set in. The leaves in the woods turned yellow and brown: the wind caught them and whirled them about; up in the air it looked very cold. The clouds hung low, heavy with hail and snowflakes, and on the fence perched the raven, trembling with the cold and croaking, "Caw! Caw!" The mere thought of it was enough to make anybody shiver. The poor duckling was certainly to be pitied!

One evening, when the sun was setting in all its splendor, a large flock of big handsome birds came out of the bushes. The duckling had never before seen anything quite so beautiful as these birds. They were dazzlingly white, with long supple necks—they were swans! They uttered a most uncanny cry and

spread their splendid great wings
to fly away from the cold regions, away to
warmer countries, to open lakes. They rose
so high, so very high in the air, that a strange
feeling came over the ugly little duckling as
he watched them. He turned round and round
in the water like a wheel, craned his neck to
follow their flight, and uttered a cry so loud
and strange that it frightened him.

He could not forget those noble birds, those
happy birds, and when they were lost to sight
he dived down to the bottom of the water;
then when he came up again he was quite
beside himself. He did not know what the
birds were called, nor where they were flying
to, and yet he loved them more than he had

ever loved anything. He did not envy them in the least; it would never have occurred to him to want such beauty for himself. He would have been quite content if only the ducks would have put up with him—the poor ugly creature!

And the winter grew so cold, so bitterly cold. The duckling was forced to swim about in the water to keep it from freezing altogether, but every night the opening became smaller and smaller; at last it froze so hard that the ice made cracking noises, and the duckling had to keep on paddling to prevent the opening from closing up. In the end he was exhausted and lay quite still, caught in the ice.

Early next morning a farmer came by, and when he saw him he went onto the ice, broke it with his wooden shoe, and carried him home to his wife. There the duckling revived.

The children wanted to play with him, but he thought they meant to do him harm, so he fluttered, terrified, into the milk pail, splashing the milk all over the room. The woman screamed and threw up her hands in fright. Then he flew into the butter tub, and from that into the flour barrel and out again. What a sight he was! The woman shrieked and struck at him with the tongs. Laughing and shouting, the children fell over each other trying to catch him. Fortunately the door was open, so the duckling dashed out into the bushes and lay there in the newly fallen snow, as if in a daze.

It would be too sad, however, to tell all the trouble and misery he had to suffer during that cruel winter. . . . When the sun began to shine warmly he found himself once more in the marsh among the reeds. The larks were singing—it was spring, beautiful spring!

Then suddenly he spread his wings; the sound of their whirring made him realize how much stronger they had grown, and they carried him powerfully along.

159

Before he knew it, he found himself in a great garden where the apple trees stood in bloom, and the lilac filled the air with its fragrance, bending down the long green branches over the meandering streams.

It was so lovely here, so full of the freshness of spring. And look! From out of the thicket in front of him came three beautiful white swans. They ruffled their feathers proudly and floated so lightly on the water. The duckling recognized the glorious creatures and felt a strange sadness come over him.

"I will fly near those royal birds, and they will peck me to death for daring to bring my ugly self near them. But that doesn't matter in the least! Better to be killed by them than to be bitten by the ducks, pecked by the hens, kicked by the girl in charge of the hen-run, and suffer untold agony in winter."

Then he flew into the water and swam toward the beautiful swans. They saw him and dashed at him with outspread rustling feathers. "Kill me," said the poor creature, and he bowed his head down upon the surface of the stream, expecting death. But what was this he saw mirrored in the clear water? He saw beneath him his own image, but it was no longer the image of an awkward dirty gray bird, ugly and repulsive—he himself was a swan!

161

It does not matter being born in a duck yard, if only one has lain in a swan's egg.

He felt quite glad to have been through so much trouble and adversity, for now he could fully appreciate not only his own good fortune, but also all the beauty that greeted him. The great swans swam round him and stroked him with their beaks.

Some little children came to the garden to throw bread and corn into the water, and the youngest exclaimed, "There's a new one!" And the other children chimed in, "Yes, there's a new one!" They clapped their hands, danced about, and ran to fetch their father and mother.

Bread and cake were thrown into the water, and everyone said, "The new one is the most beautiful of all! He's so young and handsome!" And the old swans bowed to him.

That made him feel quite embarrassed, and he put his head under his wing, not knowing what it was all about. An overwhelming happiness filled him, and yet he was not at all proud, for a good heart never becomes proud.

He remembered how once he had been despised and persecuted; and now he heard everyone saying that he was the most beautiful of all beautiful birds.

And the lilac bushes dipped their branches into the water before him; and the sun shone warm and mild. He rustled his feathers and held his graceful neck high, and from the depths of his heart he joyfully exclaimed, "I never dreamt that so much happiness was possible when I was the ugly duckling."

GLOSSARY

In this glossary, you'll find definitions for words that you may not know but that are in the stories you've read. You'll find the meaning of each word as it is used in the story. The word may have other meanings as well, which you can find in a dictionary if you're interested. If you don't find a word here that you are wondering about, go to your dictionary for help.

absolute: Something is **absolute** when it is complete or total. *Your teacher might ask for* ***absolute*** *silence during a test.*

abuelo: Spanish for "grandfather."

admires: To **admire** something is to look at it with pleasure or respect. *My friend always* ***admires*** *the cakes in the bakery window. The boy* ***admires*** *how his big brother can do tricks on his skateboard.*

adversity: Great difficulty or suffering. *The rain caused* ***adversity*** *for the campers trying to start a fire.*

agony: A feeling of great mental or physical pain. *The soccer player cried out in* **agony** *when he broke his arm.*

aloof: You are **aloof** when you keep to yourself and show little interest in others. *The new boy is* **aloof***; we're not sure whether he wants to be friends with us.*

ambled: To **amble** is to walk slowly because you aren't in a hurry. *We* **ambled** *through the park on the first day of spring, stopping a few times to pick flowers.*

amiably: If you do something **amiably**, you do it in a friendly, happy way. *My neighbor always smiles and replies* **amiably** *when I say hello to him.*

antics: Actions that are funny or silly. *Your* **antics** *in class might make your friends laugh, but they could get you in trouble with the teacher.*

anxiously: Saying or doing something **anxiously** means you feel nervous, worried, or fearful about what might happen. *The students waited* **anxiously** *to find out if they had gotten parts in the school play. "I think my dog is missing," the boy said* **anxiously***.*

appallingly: Something **appalling** fills you with shock, fear, and dislike. *The movie was so* **appallingly** *violent that we left before the end.*

166

aristocratic: People who are **aristocratic** are thought to be important or special because of their family history and are often rich or powerful. *In **aristocratic** houses, servants usually do all the cooking and cleaning.*

assured: When you **assure** someone, you tell him or her something in a very strong and sure way to take away any doubt or worry. *I **assured** my upset friend that everything was going to be fine.*

astonished: You are **astonished** when you are very surprised by something. *You might be **astonished** if your mother served you ice cream for breakfast.*

barely: If you **barely** do something, you hardly do it at all. *She was so tired after running the race that she could **barely** walk to the car.*

benachin: A dish from West Africa that contains rice, vegetables, spices, and usually some type of meat.

beseech: To make a strong request or beg for something. *I **beseeched** my parents to let me go to the party.*

bestowed: To **bestow on** or **bestow upon** is to give something (usually a gift or a prize) to someone. *She had many presents **bestowed upon** her because it was her birthday.*

bounded: To **bound** is to move quickly by taking big, jumping steps. *My dog **bounded** after the ball when I threw it.*

boundless: Something that is **boundless** has no limits or borders, or is very great in size. *The playful puppy has **boundless** energy and never wants to rest.*

brazier: A small heater that uses lighted coals and can be moved from room to room.

briskly: When you do something **briskly**, you do it quickly and with a lot of energy. *You might walk **briskly** to the bus stop if you were late for school.*

brooding: When a bird sits on its eggs until they hatch.

buenos días: Spanish for "good morning" or "good day."

buffeted: When something is **buffeted**, it is shaken around or hit many times. *The little boat was **buffeted** so much by the waves that it almost sank.*

butt of, the: If someone is **the butt of** something, it means that he or she is the target for people's jokes or mean words. *He wore a costume to school even though it wasn't Halloween, so he became **the butt of** all our jokes that day.*

campesinos: A Spanish word for people who live in the country.

camphor tree: A large evergreen tree from China and Japan that is used for oil and wood.

campo: Spanish for "countryside."

carp: A fish that lives in ponds, lakes, and slow streams.

chico: Spanish for "boy."

chiles: Small, spicy peppers that are red or green.

companionship: Friendship or good company. *Without **companionship**, long car rides can be very boring.*

compound: A group of homes with a fence or wall around them.

concentration: The act of paying very close attention to something. *Solving the puzzle took so much **concentration** that I didn't hear the doorbell ring.*

conductor: The person who leads the singing or playing of a choir, orchestra, or band. *The musicians waited quietly for the **conductor** to tell them to start.*

consequently: As a result of something, or because of something. *I jumped in a puddle; **consequently**, my shoes were soaked with dirty water.*

constantly: All the time, or without stopping. *My baby sister was crying **constantly** last night, so I didn't get any sleep.*

craned his neck: When you **crane your neck**, you stretch it up or sideways to try and see something better. *He was sitting at the back of the room, so he **craned his neck** to see over people's heads.*

daze: If you are in a **daze**, you feel so confused that you don't know what to say or do. *I was in such a **daze** that I could only sit and stare.*

dazzlingly: Something **dazzling** is very bright and almost blinding. *The snow was so **dazzlingly** white that it hurt our eyes.*

declared: You **declare** something when you say it openly and strongly. *The team captain **declared** that he was in charge and that his team had to listen to him.*

decline: If you **decline** something, you say "no" to it in a polite way. *The family decided to **decline** the invitation to the party since they already had plans.*

delicacy: A **delicacy** is something good to eat that is rare or expensive. *Caviar (fish eggs) is considered a **delicacy**—it can cost six hundred dollars a pound!*

demanded: To **demand** is to order something to be done or to ask for something firmly. *My father **demanded** that we stop playing in the mud and clean ourselves off at once.*

densest: Something is **dense** if it is crowded or thick. *In the **densest** fog, you can only see a few feet in front of you.*

desolate: When you feel **desolate**, you feel unhappy and lonely at the same time. *You might feel **desolate** if you had to move away and leave all of your friends.*

despised: Hated. *The students **despised** school lunches, so they brought food from home.*

disguised: If you are **disguised**, you have changed your looks or dress so no one knows who you are. *The movie star did not want to be disturbed, so she went shopping **disguised** with a wig and sunglasses.*

disposing: When you **dispose** of something, you get rid of it. *We spent our last few minutes at the campground **disposing** of all our trash.*

disposition: How a person usually feels and acts. *My friend has a pleasant **disposition**; he is always nice to other people.*

distinction: A **distinction** is an honor or award given to someone for being or doing something excellent. *She won first prize at the science fair, which is a great **distinction**.*

Don: A Spanish word used with an older man's first name to show respect.

Doña: A Spanish word used with an older woman's first name to show respect.

drake: A male duck.

dreadful: Very bad; awful. *The student was sent to the principal's office because of his **dreadful** behavior.*

echoed: To **echo** is to repeat or copy a sound or something someone says. *I asked my mom for cookies first, then my little sister **echoed** my question and our mom gave us both two.*

elegant: Something or someone **elegant** is stylish or graceful. *For my grandmother's birthday, we went to dinner at an **elegant** restaurant. The ballerina is a very **elegant** dancer.*

emerged: To **emerge** is to come out of a place where you were hidden. *My cat **emerged** from underneath the bed when I called for him.*

esteemed: An **esteemed** person is someone whom others respect and look up to. *A teacher who is trusted and loved by all her students is an* ***esteemed*** *teacher.*

exasperation: When you feel **exasperation**, you are very annoyed because someone or something is bothering you. *My father feels* ***exasperation*** *when people talk loudly on their phones in a movie theater.*

exquisite: Something **exquisite** is very beautiful or very finely made. *A pink and orange sunset over the ocean is* ***exquisite***. *The* ***exquisite*** *pattern on her coat was made by hand.*

fate: Some people believe that **fate** is the force that decides what happens in life and how things will turn out. *Even though she had studied for the test, she still felt her* ***fate*** *was to get a bad grade.*

ferocious: Very wild, rough, or strong. *A hungry tiger can be a* ***ferocious*** *animal. The loud, pounding music gave me a* ***ferocious*** *headache.*

fiercely: In a powerful, nasty, or mean way. *When the dog growled* ***fiercely***, *I was afraid he might bite me.*

forlornly: Someone or something acting **forlornly** is sad because it feels lonely or has been left alone. *When his mother left the room, the puppy began to cry* ***forlornly***.

gazed: To **gaze** is to look at something for a long time, especially something very beautiful or amazing. *The child* ***gazed*** *at the colorful butterflies gathered around the flowers.*

gleamed, gleaming: Something that **gleams** shines brightly. *The freshly fallen snow* ***gleamed*** *in the sun. I cleaned the silverware until it was* ***gleaming***.

glorious: Beautiful and wonderful. *It was a* ***glorious*** *spring day, so we played outside all afternoon.*

gossip: Talk about other people's personal business. ***Gossip*** *can be harmful if the stories that are being told are mean or are not true.*

grateful: If you feel **grateful**, you feel full of thanks because someone did you a favor or something made you happy. *After hiking for hours, the man was* ***grateful*** *to lie down and sip a cool drink.*

grubbed out: When plants are **grubbed out**, they are dug up by the roots so they cannot grow back.

gusto: If you do something with **gusto**, you do it with energy and excitement. *I sang with such **gusto** at the concert that I might have lost my voice!*

haggled: To **haggle** is to bargain over the price of something. *The customer **haggled** with the salesperson to try and get a better deal on the car.*

haughty: If you are **haughty**, you are very proud and look down on others. *The **haughty** student thought he was smarter than all his classmates and wouldn't be friends with anyone.*

hoarse: If someone's voice is **hoarse**, it has a rough, harsh sound. *It is hard to talk when I am sick because my voice is so **hoarse**.*

hoisted: You **hoist** something when you lift or pull it up. *The crane **hoisted** heavy pieces of metal into the air.*

huddled: You **huddle** by pulling your legs and arms close to your body. *The boy **huddled** behind the building to get out of the cold wind.*

humbly: When you do something **humbly**, you do it with respect and without pride. *The soldiers **humbly** saluted the president as he walked by them.*

impatience: When you show **impatience**, you are annoyed or angry that something is taking longer than you think it should. *You would show **impatience** if you repeated "Are we there yet?" on a long car ride.*

imported: Brought over from another country. *The fancy watches were **imported** from Switzerland.*

insistent: Something **insistent** is repeated and hard to ignore. *The fly made an **insistent** buzz in the quiet room. Because of my father's **insistent** nagging, I finally cleaned up my room.*

intently: When you do something **intently**, you give it your full attention. *The basketball player looked **intently** at the hoop as he prepared to shoot the ball.*

jabbering: To **jabber** is to talk very fast or in a way that is hard to understand. *He was so excited that he was **jabbering** away without answering any of our questions.*

kernels: Grains or seeds of corn, wheat, or other plants.

king me: A phrase used in checkers when a player reaches the other side of the board.

kowtowed: **Kowtowing** is the Chinese custom of kneeling and touching your head to the ground to show that you respect someone or something.

lacquer: A liquid that is put on a surface (like wood or metal) and dries into a smooth, shiny coating. *Lacquer is used on some types of furniture as well as on plates and bowls.*

lickety-split: A phrase that means "very quickly."

lumbered: To **lumber** is to move in a slow, heavy way. *Carrying two large suitcases, my father **lumbered** up the stairs.*

manage: To **manage** is to succeed at doing something. *That plant only gets watered once a week, but somehow it **manages** to stay alive.* To **manage** also means to control or handle something. *We need a good coach to **manage** the baseball team next year.*

marsh: A low, soft, wet area of land.

meager: If something is **meager**, there is very little or not enough of it. *I feel cranky later in the day if I eat a **meager** breakfast. The farmer's **meager** harvest of vegetables was not enough to sell at the market.*

meandering: Something that is **meandering** takes a twisting and turning path. *A **meandering** river looks like a long, winding snake if you see it from above.*

177

melodious: A sound that is **melodious** is pleasant to hear. *The sound of a church bell ringing is* **melodious**. *A good storyteller might have a* **melodious** *voice.*

miserable: Very unhappy or uncomfortable. *After his best friend moved away, my brother was* **miserable**. *Having a bad cold can make you feel* **miserable**.

monastery: A place where monks (religious men) live and work together.

much obliged: Saying "**much obliged**" means that you are thankful for something a person has done for you, and that you owe that person a favor in return. *"**Much obliged**," my neighbor said after I raked his front yard.*

muffled: A **muffled** noise is quiet and unclear because something is blocking or softening the sound. *The boy's voice was* **muffled** *by his thick winter scarf.*

muttered: To **mutter** is to talk so softly that you almost cannot be heard. *I* **muttered** *my thoughts about the movie to my friend so that I wouldn't bother the others watching it.*

of their own accord: When things happen **of their own accord**, they happen without being forced. *Your heart beats* **of its own accord**— *you don't have to make it beat.*

overwhelming: Something **overwhelming** is very strong or powerful and is hard to fight against. *She was filled with such **overwhelming** sadness that she burst into tears. The noise of the fire engine was so **overwhelming** I had to cover my ears.*

pandemonium: Noisy confusion. *When all five of my little brothers and sisters are screaming, it's **pandemonium**!*

particularly: More than usual. *My sister loves all animals, but she is **particularly** interested in birds.*

peerless: Something **peerless** is so special and wonderful that it doesn't compare to anything else. *My grandma's apple pie is **peerless**—I have never tasted a pie that is better than hers.*

persecuted: If you are **persecuted**, you are treated very badly, over and over. *Last year I was **persecuted** by the bullies in my class.*

phonograph: A record player.

plaintively: Saying something **plaintively** means you say it sadly and wishfully. *"I miss my mom," the camper said **plaintively** to her counselor.*

pleading, pleaded: To **plead** is to beg or ask for something with all your heart. *The children kept **pleading** for ice cream until their babysitter gave in.*

plucking: If you **pluck** something, you pull it with short, quick pulls. *I keep **plucking** cat hairs off of my sweater.*

plunge: To **plunge** is to fall into something very fast, without much control. *You might **plunge** into sadness if all your friends were suddenly mean to you. I am scared to jump off the high dive and **plunge** into the water.*

prosperous: People are **prosperous** if they have lots of money and success. *The owner of the bank seems **prosperous** because he wears nice suits.*

pronounce: To say words or sounds in a certain way. *We **pronounce** the word "tomato" differently—I say "to-MAY-to" and you say "toh-MAH-to."*

quaked: Shook or trembled. *My dog **quaked** during the storm, but he calmed down when I started petting him.*

quarreling: To **quarrel** is to fight or disagree angrily with someone. *The brothers are **quarreling** over whose turn it is to do the dishes.*

quivering: To **quiver** is to tremble just a little bit. *The leaves were **quivering** on the tree from the wind blowing through them. Whenever she was upset she spoke with a **quivering** voice.*

ragged: Something **ragged** is old, torn, or worn out. *My favorite jacket is becoming **ragged**; there are holes in both the elbows.*

ransacked: If a place has been **ransacked**, it has been completely (and sometimes messily) searched, sometimes by someone looking for things to steal. *My room looked as if it had been **ransacked**—there were clothes and books everywhere.*

replaced: You **replace** something by putting a new one in place of the old one. *I broke my mom's favorite dish, so I **replaced** it with a new one.* You can also **replace** something by putting it back where it belongs. *After I finished reading, I **replaced** the book on the shelf.*

repulsive: Something **repulsive** is very unpleasant or disgusting. *The rotten fruit had a **repulsive** smell.*

resemble: If you **resemble** someone or something, you look like that person or thing. *Everyone says I **resemble** my mother because we have the same hair and eye color.*

resentment: Anger or hard feelings toward someone. *She felt **resentment** toward her neighbor when he broke her window and didn't apologize.*

resist: To **resist** is to fight against a force or an action. *I tried to **resist** the cold by wearing a scarf, a hat, and mittens.*

resumed: To **resume** is to continue an activity again after stopping. *After the thunderstorm stopped, the soccer teams **resumed** play.*

revived: To **revive** something is to give new strength or life to it. *The plants were dying in the cold, but bringing them indoors **revived** them.*

salsa: A spicy sauce made of tomatoes, onions, and hot peppers.

sauntered: If you **saunter**, you walk in an easy, slow way. *If I'm not in a rush, I like to **saunter** through the park.*

savory: Something **savory** is very tasty. *We were full and happy after eating such a **savory** meal.* A **savory** dish can also be salty or strong-tasting. *Bacon is a **savory** food; so is spicy chili or curry.*

scoffed: To **scoff** is to say something in a stuck-up or snobby way. *"I never would have let that happen the way he did," she **scoffed**.*

scowling: A **scowl** is an angry frown. *The woman next door was **scowling** and shaking her fist at us because we were playing loud music.*

scrolls: Rolls of paper or parchment (specially prepared animal skin) with writing on it. *Each end of a **scroll** is usually wrapped around a rod.*

scurried: Animals or people **scurry** when they move with light, quick steps. *A squirrel might **scurry**, but an elephant wouldn't! She **scurried** down the block so she wouldn't be late for the bus.*

sensible: People who are **sensible** think things through before making decisions. *The **sensible** boy looked carefully for cars before crossing the street.*

shrieking: Making a loud, high-pitched scream or a cry. *The seagulls began **shrieking** when they saw fish in the water.*

shrine: A **shrine** is a place created to honor someone or something. *People often pray or light candles at a **shrine**.*

shriveled: Something that is **shriveled** is wrinkled and has shrunk, often because it is dried out. *When it didn't rain for a week, the plant's leaves looked **shriveled**.*

sí: Spanish for "yes."

snarling: An animal **snarls** when it growls and shows its teeth. *The mean dog sits in the yard **snarling** at anyone who walks by.*

183

snickered: To **snicker** is to quietly laugh in a nasty way. *The boy **snickered** rudely when the substitute teacher tried to make a joke.*

snubbed: To **snub** someone means that you pay no attention to that person or treat him or her without respect. *My friend **snubbed** me by walking past me in the hall and pretending not to see me.*

solemn: Very serious. *You might make a **solemn** promise never to lie to your mother. The graduation was a very **solemn** event, so everyone had to dress up and be very polite.*

sombreros: A **sombrero** is a hat with a wide brim. ***Sombreros** are often made of straw and are worn in Mexico and the southwestern part of the United States.*

soughing: Making a sighing, moaning, or soft rustling sound. **Sough** can rhyme with "cow" or "cuff."

splendor: Great beauty or grandness. *The crowd clapped and cheered at the **splendor** of the fireworks display.*

spunk: Courage and spirit. *It takes **spunk** to speak up about something you believe in when you know that others don't agree.*

squinted: When you **squint**, you partly close your eyes, either to avoid a bright light or to see something better. *We **squinted** when we came out into the sunlight after being in the dark movie theater. The librarian **squinted**, trying to read the tiny words on the page.*

stifling: If something is **stifling**, it causes you to have trouble breathing because it is too hot or there isn't enough air. *A room might be **stifling** if someone shut all the windows and turned the heat up very high.*

stricken: When you are **stricken**, you are in great pain, fright, or shock from something that has happened. *You might be **stricken** if you saw a car accident or heard someone scream in the middle of the night.*

strolling: To **stroll** is to walk in a slow, easy way. *I went **strolling** down the hall to my classroom since I had plenty of time to get there.*

strut: To **strut** means to walk proudly and stiffly, usually because you are showing off or trying to impress someone. *He began to **strut** around the room, showing everyone the medal he won in the race.*

185

stunned: When you are **stunned**, you are so surprised that you don't know what to do. *We were so **stunned** that we'd won the contest that we just stared at one another. The class was **stunned** and sad when they were told that their teacher would not be returning after winter break.*

sumptuous: Something **sumptuous** is very grand and looks expensive. *A delicious meal with twenty different dishes would be **sumptuous**.*

superior: Better or finer than other people or things. *Fresh fish from the ocean is **superior** to the kind you buy in a can.* When people act **superior**, they act as if they are better than everyone else. *At the restaurant, he ordered the waiter around in a **superior** way.*

supple: Something **supple** bends and moves easily. *Dancers need to have **supple** bodies in order to stretch and leap into the air.*

swollen: If something is **swollen**, it has grown in size, and it might look puffy or unusually large. *After I smashed my finger with a hammer, it became **swollen** to twice its size.*

sympathetically: If you say something **sympathetically**, you say it as if you understand and share the other person's feelings. *"My cat ran away once, too," my neighbor said **sympathetically** as we searched for my lost pet.*

symphony: A long piece of classical music played by many different instruments. A **symphony** usually has several different sections, or *movements.*

tatami: A straw mat that covers the floor of a Japanese home.

tedious: Something **tedious** is tiring because it is boring or slow or because it takes a long time. *It might be hard to stay awake during a **tedious** movie.*

thicket: An area where plants, bushes, or small trees grow close together. *The chipmunk ran into a **thicket** of leafy bushes so the fox wouldn't see him.*

tortilla: A round, flat Mexican bread made from corn or flour.

transplanted: To **transplant** a tree or a plant is to dig it up and plant it somewhere else. *We **transplanted** the raspberry bush from the backyard to the front yard.*

uncanny: Something **uncanny** is unusual and a little bit strange. *The wind was howling in an* **uncanny** *way, giving the night a creepy feel. My sister has an* **uncanny** *sense of direction and somehow knows her way around in a strange place.*

uneasy: Someone who is feeling **uneasy** is worried or troubled. *The boy became* **uneasy** *when he couldn't find his puppy.*

urgently: When you say or do something **urgently**, you say or do it in a way to make people pay attention to you and respond quickly. *"Everyone needs to follow me right now," the teacher said* **urgently** *when the fire alarm rang.*

uttered: To **utter** is to speak or to make other sounds with your voice. *He* **uttered** *a shout of pain when someone stepped on his foot.*

vague: Unclear. *You can see only* **vague** *shapes of things when it's foggy or dark outside.*

venerable: Worthy of respect because of age, knowledge, or position in life. *My grandparents are* **venerable** *because they are older and wiser than I.*

virtuous: Being a **virtuous** person means that you are good, honest, or trustworthy. *I know that my brother is* **virtuous** *because he always does the right thing when he has to make tough decisions.*

wandering: To **wander** is to move about with no real place you need to be. *When my friends and I have a free afternoon, we spend it **wandering** around the park by my house.*

wattles: The loose, wrinkled skin hanging down from a turkey's throat.

wearily: When you do something **wearily**, you do it in a tired, worn-out way. *After running the long race, the girl walked **wearily** home.*

weave: To **weave** through something means to move in a zig-zagging, winding way. *You **weave** through a crowd of people to get to the door.* To **weave** also means to crisscross strips or threads of material in a pattern to make something larger, such as a piece of cloth.

whetstone: A stone used for sharpening knives or other blades.

windfall: A piece of sudden good luck that you don't expect. *It would be quite a **windfall** to win the lottery.*

wretched: Something **wretched** is in very bad shape. *My **wretched** umbrella started leaking the minute I went out into the rain.*

ACKNOWLEDGMENTS

All possible care has been taken to trace ownership and secure permission for each selection in this series. The Great Books Foundation wishes to thank the following authors, publishers, and representatives for permission to reproduce copyrighted material:

BOUNDLESS GRACE, by Mary Hoffman. Copyright © 1995 by Mary Hoffman. Reproduced by permission of Dial Books for Young Readers, a division of Penguin Group (USA), Inc.

THE SCAREBIRD, by Sid Fleischman. Copyright © 1987 by Sid Fleischman. Reproduced by permission of the estate of the author.

CHIN YU MIN AND THE GINGER CAT, by Jennifer Armstrong. Copyright © 1993 by Jennifer Armstrong. Reproduced by permission of Random House Children's Books, a division of Random House, Inc.

THE GOLD COIN, by Alma Flor Ada, translated by Bernice Randall. Copyright © 1991 by Alma Flor Ada. Reproduced by permission of Simon & Schuster, Inc.

The Magic Listening Cap, from THE MAGIC LISTENING CAP: MORE TALES FROM JAPAN, by Yoshiko Uchida. Copyright © 1955 by Yoshiko Uchida. Reproduced by permission of the Bancroft Library, University of California, Berkeley.

THE MUSHROOM MAN, by Ethel Pochocki. Copyright © 1993 by Ethel Pochocki. Reproduced by permission of Tillbury House.

THE BANZA, by Diane Wolkstein. Copyright © 1978, 1981 by Diane Wolkstein. Reproduced by permission of the author.

THE UPSIDE-DOWN BOY, by Juan Felipe Herrera. Copyright © 2000 by Juan Felipe Herrera. Originally published by Children's Book Press. Reproduced by permission of Lee & Low Books, Inc.

ILLUSTRATION CREDITS

Caroline Binch's illustrations for *Boundless Grace* are from the book of the same name, by Mary Hoffman. Copyright © 1995 by Caroline Binch. Reproduced by permission of Dial Books for Young Readers, a division of Penguin Group (USA), Inc.

Barbara McClintock prepared the illustrations for *The Scarebird*.

Carll Cnuet prepared the illustrations for *Chin Yu Min and the Ginger Cat*.

Rosalind Kaye prepared the illustrations for *The Gold Coin*.

Ed Young prepared the illustrations for *The Magic Listening Cap*.

Barry Moser's illustrations for *The Mushroom Man* are from the book of the same name, by Ethel Pochocki. Copyright © 1993 by Barry Moser. Reproduced by permission of Tillbury House.

Rosalind Kaye prepared the illustrations for *The Banza*.

Carll Cneut prepared the illustrations for *The Upside-Down Boy*.

Omar Rayyan prepared the illustrations for *The Ugly Duckling*.

Cover art by Rich Lo. Copyright © 2014 by Rich Lo.

Design by THINK Book Works.

TAKING NOTES AND
HIGHLIGHTING

Taking notes and highlighting will help you remember what you were
thinking while reading a story. Be sure to mark:

Anything that seems important/

Anything that surprises you X

Anything that puzzles you ?

Anything you like

Anything you don't like

Anything that doesn't seem right

Anything seen OVER and OVER again